65 WAYS TO USE MANGOSTEEN JUICE

For your Better Health

Easy Step-by-Step Ideas for Oral Procedures and
Topical and Internal Applications of Garcinia Mangostana

Isa Navarre

**65 Ways to Use Mangosteen Juice for Your Better Health
Easy Step-by-Step Ideas for Oral Procedures and
Topical and Internal Applications and Procedures for
*Garcinia Mangostana***

Copyright © 2003 Isa Navarre

All rights reserved. No part of this book may be reproduced, stored in a retrieval system, or transmitted in any form by any means, whether electronic, mechanical, photocopying, recording, or otherwise, without prior written permission of the copyright holder. For information address:

Direct Source Publishing
15 East 400 South
Orem, UT 84058

Typesetting and cover design by: Shane Allman Art & Design
Back cover photo by: Robert Norman photography

IMPORTANT NOTICE

The information in this book is designed to provide health information for purposes of reference and guidance and to accompany, not replace, the services of a qualified health care practitioner or physician. It is not the intent of the author or publisher to prescribe any substance to cure, mitigate, treat, or prevent any disease. In the event you use this information with or without seeking medical attention, the author and publisher shall not be liable or otherwise responsible for any loss, damage or injury caused or arising out of, directly or indirectly, by the information contained in this book or its use.

Printed in the United States of America.

1-887938-50-8

For those who see the beauty of nature, who revel in the peace and serenity it provides and who appreciate and enjoy the bountiful gifts of nutritional and therapeutic products it so selflessly offers to all.

Table of Contents

Introduction i
How to use this book iii
SECTION 1: Drinking Applications 1
   1. Your First Dose 3
   2. Evaluating the Immediate Effects of Mangosteen 7
   3. Gradually Introducing Mangosteen to Your Diet 11
   4. The Loading Dose 15
   5. Sipping Mangosteen 19
   6. Drinking Mangosteen All at Once 21
   7. The Maintenance Dose #1 23
   8. The Maintenance Dose #2 27
   9. The Maintenance Dose #3 29
  10. A Procedure for Acute Conditions 33
  11. A Procedure for Chronic Conditions 37
  12. A Procedure for Health Improvement #1 39
  13. A Procedure for Health Improvement #2 41
  14. A Technique for Stubborn Conditions 45
  15. The Top Dose Procedure 49
  16. The Anti-Stress Procedure 53
  17. The Trauma Dose 57
  18. The Sick-Day Prevention Dose 59
  19. Taking Mangosteen with Herbs and Supplements 61
  20. The Mangosteen Chinese Body Clock Procedure 63
  21. Interrupting Mangosteen Therapy 67
  22. Locating Mangosteen's Healing Target 71
  23. Mangosteen Tea 75
  24. A Mangosteen Decoction 79
  25. The Mangosteen Tonic 83
  26. The Mangosteen Fast #1 85
  27. The Mangosteen Fast #2 89
  28. The Mangosteen Detoxification Program 93
  29. Adding Mangosteen to Recipes 97
  30. Giving Mangosteen to Children 103
  31. Giving Mangosteen to Pets 107
  32. Keeping Mangosteen a Family Friend 113
  33. Sharing a First Dose with Others 117

SECTION 2: Topical Applications of Mangosteen 121
    34. Mangosteen Abdominal Conditioner 123
    35. Mangosteen Astringent and Aftershave 127
    36. Mangosteen Analgesic Ointment 131
    37. Mangosteen Clay 135
    38. Mangosteen for Cuticle Care 139
    39. Mangosteen Deodorant 141
    40. Mangosteen Exfoliating Lotion 145
    41. Mangosteen Eye Poultice .149
    42. Mangosteen First Aid for Minor Wounds 153
    43. Mangosteen Foot Treatment 157
    44. Mangosteen Hand and Body Lotion 161
    45. Mangosteen Hemorrhoid Treatments 163
    46. Mangosteen Massage Oil .167
    47. Mangosteen Mini-Poultice 169
    48. Mangosteen Nail Treatment 171
    49. Mangosteen Paste 173
    50. The Mangosteen Poultice .179
    51. Mangosteen Rash Plaster .183
    52. Mangosteen Scalp Treatment 187
    53. Mangosteen Sitz Bath 189
    54. Mangosteen Sunburn Treatment 191
    55. The Easy Mangosteen Skin Conditioner 195
    56. Mangosteen Toe Treatment 197

SECTION 3: Internal Applications of Mangosteen 199
    57. The Auto-Distribution Dose 201
    58. The Mangosteen Enema .203
    59. The Mangosteen Gargle 207
    60. The Mangosteen Mouthwash 209
    61. The Oral Detox 213
    62. The Mangosteen Rectal Implant 217
    63. The Tooth and Gum Compress 221
    64. The Tooth and Gum Pack .223
    65. Mangosteen Vaginal Wipe 225
Appendix 1: Health Evaluation Questionnaire 227
Appendix 2: Cleansing Reactions 233
Appendix 3: What if Mangosteen Doesn't Seem to Work for Me? .241
Appendix 4: What if My Symptoms Return? 245

INDEX: 249

Introduction

"This tastes too good to be good for you," I said to myself after trying mangosteen juice for the first time. Mangosteen is a delicious and medicinal tropical fruit known to traditional Asian healers for centuries, but new to the Western marketplace. My attitude about mangosteen's taste persisted until I began to read pages of testimonials of sincere, grateful people who had enjoyed results from mangosteen after nothing else had helped. Some of these results were miraculous, and overall, their scope was mind-boggling. People were being helped with acute and long-standing conditions, systemic and topical ailments, as well as incurable diseases and common malaise. Now I just *had* to find out: How could something that tasted so good be so good for you?

My answer unfolded as I studied recent publications and internet articles on mangosteen. My favorite, an excellent little book by J. Frederic Templeman, M.D., entitled, *Mangosteen The X-Factor*, clearly summarizes the science behind mangosteen. Dr. Templeman explains that mangosteen contains a variety of "phytoceuticals" (plant-based substances with medicinal potential that I like to call "healing compounds"). These healing compounds have been widely studied by medical and pharmacological researchers who have found solid evidence to support the personal experiences of mangosteen users.*

A Sound Concepts publication, *Mangosteen: Asia's Ancient Ambrosia for Better Health* (Orem, UT: Sound Concepts, 2003, pages 12-15), explains some of the research behind four of the many significant healing compounds of mangosteen. These include polysaccharides, quinones, stilbenes and xanthones (at least two dozen xanthones are found in mangosteen). Briefly, polysaccharides have anti-cancer and anti-bacterial effects. Quinones have cancer-fighting properties and are strong free radical inhibitors. Stilbenes, which are anti-fungal compounds, seem to be helpful for cancer and heart disease and for positively affecting cholesterol levels. And finally, the highly active xanthones, which seem to be the most exciting class of healing compounds in mangosteen, have anti-viral, anti-fungal, anti-bacterial, anti-oxidant, anti-depressant, anti-inflammatory, anti-histaminic and anti-ulcer effects.

---

* Templeman, J. Frederic, M.D., *Mangosteen the X-Factor*, (Orem, UT: Sound Concepts), 2002, p. 8.

I should add that Mangosteen also contains nutrients essential for our diet. These nutrients include potassium, calcium, phosphorous, iron and vitamins B1, B2, B6 and vitamin C.*

Talk about a pharmacy in a bottle!

Yet none of these effects mean anything unless you can enjoy them yourself. I have always believed in the value and necessity of personal investigation, especially when deciding whether to add something to your diet or lifestyle. So give mangosteen a try. Use this book to find ways to use mangosteen that best suit your condition and to make your mangosteen experience as positive and pleasant as possible. Let your personal evaluation speak for itself. Discover how something that tastes so good can, indeed, be good for you!

---

* Templeman, p. 10.

How to Use This Book

I have divided the sixty-five ways to use mangosteen that are described in this book into three sections. Section 1 covers different procedures and techniques for drinking mangosteen. Section 2 describes topical uses and Section 3 introduces techniques for taking mangosteen internally.

Each of the chapters in this book are also divided into three parts. First, I suggest some conditions that might be aided by the application that the chapter describes. These are conditions gleaned from testimonials I found on the internet and in various publications, as well as from personal experience. This list is given for educational purposes and is not meant to provide medical advice or to be used as a prescription.

In the second part of each chapter, I give detailed, step-by-step instructions on how to do each mangosteen application. In the third part, I offer additional helpful information about the procedure. Some of the procedures in this book are very simple, and others are more involved. All in all, they should appeal to a variety of people and be helpful for a variety of needs.

At the back of the book, you'll find four appendices. The first one contains the essential Health Evaluation Questionnaire and instructions for finding your Health Index. Your Health Index is based on the results of the questionnaire. It is a numerical value that rates your current state of health. It is very easy to calculate and can help you objectively evaluate how well mangosteen has been working for you. The second appendix discusses "cleansing reactions," including how to know if you're having one and what to do about it. And Appendices 3 and 4 cover some of the questions and concerns people might have as they progress on their road to health.

Finally, the detailed index at the back of the book can help you find the applications and procedures that might be helpful to you. Look up your health concerns in the index and refer to the pages listed.

As you read this book, keep in mind that I am not a physician. The ideas that I offer for using mangosteen are not meant to replace your doctor's advice. I simply wanted to share what I know about liquid nutritional supplements and what I and others have experienced with mangosteen, so that you can have the opportunity to benefit from this amazing and special gift of nature.

Enjoy!

SECTION 1
Drinking Applications

Mangosteen is a "functional" fruit juice. This means it offers more than the ordinary fruit juice beverage. Much more. In fact, mangosteen packs so many healing compounds that it should not be taken by the glassful like other juice beverages. Most people need only one or two ounces of mangosteen a day. Of course, how many ounces of mangosteen that are right for you depends on your health condition and the way your body uniquely responds to mangosteen. The following chapters will help you decide just how much mangosteen you might need.

Section 1 offers a variety of procedures and techniques for drinking mangosteen. There should be something for everyone, including children, teens, pets, athletes, relatively healthy individuals as well as the seriously ill. Please read through the chapters to learn about the scope of mangosteen and the possibilities for its use. Choose one health challenge to work on first, and then decide which Drinking Applications seem most appropriate for that condition. Then experiment. You are welcome to modify the guidelines and dosages I've suggested to suit your individual needs. Continue with the applications and procedures you have chosen for at least three months. At the same time, peruse Sections 2 and 3 to find topical and internal applications of mangosteen that will also help your condition. Use them freely.

I have tried to organize the chapters in this section as logically as possible, however they are not alphabetical. Earmark the table of contents so you can easily refer to it in order to find the chapters you use the most.

Section 1: Drinking Applications

1.
Your First Dose

The instructions in this chapter explain how to get the most and best from your first dose of mangosteen—and every dose thereafter.

TAKE YOUR FIRST DOSE:

- When you have made a commitment to improve your health, and would like to see if mangosteen will help you achieve your health goals.
- When you are convinced that mangosteen juice might help you, either because you've read some of the extensive scientific research on it and/or heard compelling testimonials from others.
- When you have completed a copy of the Health Evaluation Questionnaire in Appendix 1 (page 227).
- When you have read Chapter 3 on Evaluating the Immediate Effects of Mangosteen. You might want to use the techniques described in that chapter when taking your first dose.

**HOW TO TAKE A
FIRST DOSE OF MANGOSTEEN:**

Decide on an amount of mangosteen juice to start with. The usual amount for a first dose is one to two tablespoonfuls (one-half to one ounce). If you are concerned that your body might be sensitive to mangosteen juice, please read Chapter 3, Gradually Introducing Mangosteen to Your Diet. Based on what you learn in that chapter, modify the amount of your first dose if necessary.

1. Shake the bottle of mangosteen.

    Turn a sealed bottle of mangosteen juice upside down. Notice the cloudy purple pulp and the tiny particles of purple rind that have settled to the bottom of the bottle. With the bottle still upside down, shake it gently until the particles are mixed throughout the juice. (Check the bottom of the bottle to make sure.) Do this every time you take mangosteen. Then your first dose from the bottle should have the same amount of mangosteen pulp and rind as the last.

2. Open the bottle and pour your dose of mangosteen.

Pour it into a measuring cup or better yet, a one-ounce plastic medicine cup. (Available at drug stores.) You can drink directly from the medicine cup or pour the dose into a drinking glass.

3. Take a sip of the mangosteen.

Hold the sip in your mouth for about five to ten seconds before swallowing. Do the same with the remainder of the dose. Whether or not this is your first dose, swirl your glass of mangosteen after each sip. This keeps the tiny pieces of rind mixed throughout the dose so that some are present in each sip that you take. If, after the first sip, you find the flavor is too tangy, mix the rest of the dose with a little water and/or fruit juice.

4. Consume the leftover rind particles.

Likely, a small amount of rind particles will be left behind. Scoop them out with a spoon or your finger and eat them. Or pour some water into the cup, swirl it to pick up the rind particles and then drink. Some people may prefer chewing the particles before swallowing. (I like to break them apart using my front teeth.)

**EQUIVALENTS HELPFUL TO KNOW
FOR THE PROCEDURES IN THIS BOOK:**

- Three Teaspoonfuls = One Tablespoonful
- Two Tablespoonfuls = One Ounce
- One Ounce = 1/8 of a Cup

MORE ABOUT YOUR FIRST DOSE:

Sip your first dose slowly, instead of drinking it all at once. This introduces your body to mangosteen's healing compounds and their effects. Try closing your eyes while sipping your first dose (see Locating Mangosteen's Healing Target on page 71). You have taken the first step on a journey to greater health, so try to appreciate the moment.

If necessary, follow each dose of mangosteen with at least a few sips of water. This will be helpful for those who are not yet accustomed to mangosteen's tanginess, or who find that the tiny flecks of mangosteen rind get stuck in their teeth. Drinking some water after taking mangosteen not only cleanses the mouth but gives you a chance to drink up those last bits of rind that usually settle on the bottom of the glass.

Indonesian folk healers treasured the mangosteen rind for its healing properties. This is why I suggest drinking every last particle of rind that settles to the bottom of your drinking glass. Shaking the mangosteen bottle before pouring some out will ensure that you get plenty of rind in each dose.

Another reason to shake your mangosteen bottle is because the watery liquid that rises to the top of the bottle is more tangy than the pulp that settles to the bottom of the bottle, which tastes sweeter. Mixing the mangosteen offsets the tanginess with the sweeter pulp.

To measure mangosteen, you could use a tablespoon-sized measuring spoon. But a one-ounce plastic medicine cup is much more convenient. You can also use a glass measuring cup that lists ounces. Hold the measuring cup at eye level to ensure an accurate amount.

Medicine Cups

Throughout this book I suggest pouring and measuring doses in one-ounce medicine cups. They are convenient and can easily be used to separate the mangosteen juice from the rind, as described in the chapter Adding Mangosteen to Recipes, as well as in many of the chapters in Sections 2 and 3. You can also drink your dose directly from a medicine cup without having to pour the dose into a glass. Medicine cups are inexpensive and you can find them in most drug stores. You might even have one already in your medicine cabinet. Cough medicines are often sold with a one-ounce medicine cup.

Section 1: Drinking Applications

2.

Evaluating the Immediate Effects of Mangosteen

Not everyone can sense mangosteen's effects right away. This procedure is worth trying to see if you can. You may be surprised!

USE THIS PROCEDURE TO:

- Gain assurance that mangosteen can help you.
- Discover how quickly mangosteen can begin to affect your body.
- Preview how and where mangosteen may help you first.
- Find out if your body will react unfavorably to mangosteen.
- Test your personal level of body awareness and sensitivity.

HOW TO EVALUATE THE
IMMEDIATE EFFECTS OF MANGOSTEEN:

1. Pour your first dose of mangosteen into a drinking glass per the instructions on pages 3-4. Be sure to shake the bottle before pouring.

2. Before you drink the mangosteen, establish some reference points that are easy to self evaluate, such as lung capacity, visual acuity and a sense of how energetic you feel. For example, take a deep breath and then exhale. This will give you a sense of your lung capacity. Look around the room at objects near and far, to assess the quality of your eyesight. Also evaluate your energy level: Are you feeling tired, energized or somewhere in between?

3. Now take a small sip of mangosteen and hold it in your mouth for about ten to twenty seconds. Meanwhile, tune in to any sensations you may be feeling in your body. Close your eyes if you want to. Then swallow. Repeat with the remainder of the mangosteen.

4. Reexamine how your body feels. Do you notice anything different?

- Take another deep breath. Are your lungs able to take in more air or is it easier to exhale without coughing? Do you feel more enlivened after taking a deep breath? Are your sinuses more open? Mangosteen is renowned for its anti-inflammatory and anti-histiminic properties.

- Look around the room. Do things appear clearer? Are colors more vivid? Mangosteen may improve cellular communication.

- Do you feel more calm and centered? Many people who live stressful lives find that mangosteen helps them relax.

- Do you feel more energized? Mangosteen may improve cellular function throughout the body.

- Do you feel warmth anywhere in your body? Mangosteen may improve circulation or else you may be feeling mangosteen's healing energy (see page 71).

- Do you feel more integrated throughout your body or a greater sense of connection with yourself? Healing substances like mangosteen help the cells access information about their true purpose—information which may have become buried or obscured by disease or free radicals.

- If you have a particular health challenge, do you notice any difference in your symptoms? You may or may not notice changes so soon. Some people need to take mangosteen for weeks or months before they enjoy significant improvements.

MORE ABOUT THE IMMEDIATE EFFECTS OF MANGOSTEEN:

When you do this procedure, be sure to take a *small* sip. Taking too much at once can make your mouth pucker if you are sensitive to, or unprepared for the tangy taste.

It will be easier to notice differences in how you feel if you do this procedure with your first dose. If you try this procedure after you have already started taking mangosteen, the difference between how you feel before and after you take a dose probably won't be as obvious. Here's why. The first time you take a health-improving substance like mangosteen, your level of health will jump to a higher plateau—whether you notice it or not. Subsequent doses will raise your level of health more gradually, or to a deeper level. Thus the changes are less obvious. Moreover, when your body receives mangosteen for the first time, it may recognize that mangosteen is filling a nutritional deficiency. You may feel better right away because unconsciously your body is telling you, "This feels good! Keep taking mangosteen. This is what I want and need!"

Changes in lung capacity, eyesight and energy level are easy for most people to notice. That is why I chose these references for this procedure. Feel free to customize this procedure by changing or modifying the questions listed above or the order in which you consider them.

Try using this procedure when you introduce mangosteen to others. Lead them through each step as they take their first drink. This can be a fun way for friends to share mangosteen with each other. (See Sharing a First Dose with Others on page 117.)

If, after taking your first dose, you have an immediate, uncomfortable reaction to mangosteen, it may be due to allergies, a toxin release or cleansing reaction, or because your body is dehydrated.

- Allergies to mangosteen are probably very rare. But some people may be allergic to the other ingredients that may be included in mangosteen juice such as: apple, pear, grape, blueberry, raspberry, strawberry, cranberry, and cherry juice.
- Keep in mind that what seems to be an allergic reaction may really be a cleansing reaction (page 233). If you have a buildup of toxins that are ready to be released, one dose of mangosteen may be just enough to invite them out.

- If your body is dehydrated, it will not be able to properly flush the toxins that mangosteen can release. The toxin buildup that ensues could cause uncomfortable symptoms that can mimic an allergic reaction.

To find out more about cleansing reactions, including how to identify them and what to do about them, please refer to page 233.

3.

Gradually Introducing Mangosteen to Your Diet

In some cases, it is wise to introduce mangosteen to your body slowly, over time.

WHEN TO GRADUALLY INTRODUCE MANGOSTEEN TO YOUR DIET:

- You have a weak or hypersensitive stomach and are concerned that mangosteen might irritate it.
- You are particularly sensitive to the effects of supplements.
- Your body is fragile in the face of change.
- You are taking prescription medications.
- You are concerned that you might be among the rare few who are allergic to one or more of the fruit juices that may be mixed with mangosteen to make its flavor more familiar to the Western palate.
- You have heavy metal poisoning or severe toxicity and are concerned that mangosteen might detoxify you too quickly and leave you with an uncomfortable cleansing reaction.
- You have an intuitive sense that your body is going to be sensitive to mangosteen.

YOU MAY PREFER TO START WITH THIS PROCEDURE IF YOU HAVE:

- Chemical poisoning.
- Conditions resulting from dehydration.
- Diabetes.
- Heavy-metal poisoning.

65 Ways to Use Mangosteen

- Mercury poisoning.
- Parasites, causing debilitation.
- Suspicion of allergy to mangosteen or one of the ingredients included in mangosteen juice.
- Systemic yeast infections.
- Toxicity in the body, causing debilitation.
- Weak or sensitive stomach.

HOW TO GRADUALLY INTRODUCE MANGOSTEEN TO YOUR DIET:

1. Start by taking one-quarter teaspoonful of mangosteen two or three times a day. Take your doses at least four to six hours apart so that your body has ample time to assimilate mangosteen's nutrients. For example, you could take one dose in the morning and one in the afternoon or evening.

Optional: Measure the mangosteen and pour it into a drinking glass. Then fill the glass with purified, spring or clean well water. Sip the dose, taking as much time as you need to finish it. You may take these doses in the form of Mangosteen Tea, Method #2, (page 76).

2. After a week, increase your dosage to one-half teaspoonful. Prepare your doses as described in Step 1.

3. Two weeks later, increase your dosage to one teaspoonful. Prepare your doses as described in Step 1.

4. Continue to increase your dosages by one-half teaspoonful every two to four weeks until you are taking a Maintenance Dose of one ounce a day. (One ounce equals six teaspoonfuls.) If you are comfortable with increasing your dosages sooner, please feel free to do so.

Note: Before pouring your dose, remember to turn the bottle of mangosteen upside down and shake it gently until the rind particles are well mixed with the rest of the juice. Because you are starting with such a small amount of mangosteen, pour your dose immediately after you have finished shaking the bottle. The pulp and rind particles fall quickly to the bottom of the bottle, and you will want to make sure that some are included in your dose.

MORE ABOUT GRADUALLY INTRODUCING MANGOSTEEN TO YOUR DIET:

Gradually increase your dosage every few days or every few weeks as your health suggests. Increase your dosage slowly as described in Step 4. If you like, you could experiment by continuing to increase your dosage to the levels suggested in other chapters. For example, see the Procedure for Chronic Conditions (page 37) and the Top Dose Procedure (page 49).

When you are measuring mangosteen, hold the measuring spoon over the drinking glass. This way, if you accidentally overfill the spoon, you can pour back the extra into the bottle. After you have measured the proper amount of mangosteen, then add the water.

This procedure starts with very low dosages of mangosteen in order to avoid unnecessary cleansing reactions. At the same time, we want to strengthen the body—slowly and gradually—so that it can withstand a natural and balanced release of toxins. A mangosteen-nourished body is not a satisfying host to yeast and parasites, which will begin to die off. Dead yeast and parasites are extremely toxic to the body. Drinking your doses with water will help flush these toxins from your system.

If drinking mangosteen makes you feel nauseated, it may be because your body is toxic, perhaps more than you may have thought. This procedure will also help your body become accustomed to mangosteen in a balanced way. Plus it supplies your diet with extra water which can help flush toxins.

If you have a buildup of mercury or other heavy metals in your mouth, also try the Oral Detox (page 213) everyday—but follow the procedure using a glassful of water with a small amount of mangosteen in it.

Drinking your small dose of mangosteen in a glass of water has side-benefits. A small amount of mangosteen in a glass of water seems to make the water more bio-available to the cells. Dehydrated cells, ironically, often resist water. Including a small amount of mangosteen in the water encourages the cells to drink.

MANGOSTEEN AND DIABETES:

Diabetics may want to follow this procedure if they are taking insulin and are concerned that mangosteen will improve their blood sugar levels too quickly. However you could start with a Maintenance Dose (page 23) or the Procedure for Chronic Conditions (page 37) as long as you check your blood sugar level frequently and modify your insulin level accordingly.

TAKING MANGOSTEEN
WITH PRESCRIPTION MEDICATIONS:

You should be able to take mangosteen along with prescription medications without problem. After all, mangosteen is simply a fruit juice. However, if you or your doctor are at all concerned about it, start with this Procedure for Gradually Introducing Mangosteen to Your Diet. Your confidence and comfort taking mangosteen should increase with each dose that you take, especially if you start to feel better.

Section 1: Drinking Applications

4.

The Loading Dose

The Loading Dose is suggested for those who are relatively healthy and planning to take a daily Maintenance Dose of Mangosteen (pages 23, 27). It is also suggested for those who have chronic conditions. After taking the Loading Dose, they should follow the Procedure for Chronic Conditions (page 37).

TRY THE LOADING DOSE TO:

- Relieve an array of nutritional deficiencies that you may have, which would take much longer to alleviate with only a Maintenance Dose (page 23).
- Saturate your body with mangosteen healing compounds in order to maximize the benefits of a subsequent Maintenance Dose.
- Test how well mangosteen will help you clear minor health conditions and alleviate the symptoms of relatively mild chronic conditions.

HOW TO TAKE THE LOADING DOSE:

1. Take two ounces (1/4 cup) of mangosteen twice a day.

    - Measure two ounces and pour it into a drinking glass. Drink it as is, or add one to eight ounces (one cup) of natural fruit juice, or add purified, spring or clean well water. Drink this all at once or sip as desired. Swirl the glass before each sip to keep the pieces of mangosteen rind dispersed throughout the dose.
    - Take your second two-ounce dose at least four to six hours after your first.

- If you are enjoying mangosteen's effects, try a third two-ounce dose.

2. Follow the Loading Dose for five or six days. This will require about one bottle of mangosteen.

MORE ABOUT THE LOADING DOSE:

Taking your two doses several hours apart gives your body time to assimilate mangosteen's nutrients and healing compounds. You could take one dose in the morning and one in the afternoon. Avoid taking a dose in the evening if you find that taking nutritional supplements at that time keeps you awake at night.

In general, teenagers can take the amount of mangosteen suggested for adults. Children from age 6 to 12 could try half the suggested dosage for adults (in this case, two ounces a day). Children under age 6 may need only one ounce a day as a loading dose.

Most children love the taste of mangosteen. However, if your children hesitate to drink it plain, add their dose to fruit juice. Then they may never know they're drinking it. But don't expect them to like the bits of mangosteen rind that will settle to the bottom of their glass. It may take some creativity to get your children to ingest them. See the chapter, Adding Mangosteen to Recipes on page 97.

A Loading Dose allows mangosteen to alleviate any sub-clinical deficiencies that you may have in mangosteen's nutrients and healing compounds before you start a Maintenance Dose. Such deficiencies can lead to a host of health complaints. Sometimes a deficiency in only a single nutrient can cause many symptoms and discomforts. After a few days on a Loading Dose, these symptoms often disappear or are significantly reduced.

Indeed, soon after you begin taking mangosteen, you may notice that you feel better overall. You may have more energy and better mental focus, or certain aches and pains may abate. Enjoy your better health for it is indeed a wonderful feeling! But keep in mind that any progress toward greater health involves cycles. The peaks of each cycle may get higher as your health improves, but they are interspersed with valleys.

These valleys represent adjustments your body is making to a healthier state, and are sometimes associated with symptoms generally classified as "cleansing reactions." (For information on cleansing reactions, see page 233.)

After only a few days on the Loading Dose, you may sense that taking four ounces a day is too much. This may be a subjective feeling but trust it. Cut back to one or two ounces on that day. The next day, try to resume the Loading regimen. However, your body may simply be trying to tell you that it has finished "loading," and that it is ready for the Maintenance Procedure.

Section 1: Drinking Applications

5.

Sipping Mangosteen

Mangosteen doses can be sipped or taken all at once. Here are some insights about sipping mangosteen.

TRY SIPPING FOR:

- Adding variety to your daily doses of mangosteen.
- Acute conditions (after you have taken a Trauma Dose).
- Chronic (ongoing) conditions.
- Conditions in which swallowing is difficult.
- Extreme illness.
- Overcoming cravings for nicotine, other addictive substances or for certain food you are trying to avoid.
- The Mangosteen Anti-Stress Procedure.
- When you want to relax and enjoy a cup of hot Mangosteen Tea, (page 75) or a glass of mangosteen iced tea.
- When you drink your mangosteen at your desk while you are working to help keep your mind sharp and your attention focused.

HOW TO SIP MANGOSTEEN:

1. Prepare your dose of mangosteen as described in one of the other procedures in this book.

2. Drink a small quantity of mangosteen and hold it in your mouth for a few seconds before swallowing. Take your time when you sip mangosteen. Separate each sip by at least a few seconds or longer.

3. Repeat Step 2 until the dose is gone.

MORE ABOUT SIPPING MANGOSTEEN:

Instead of sipping mangosteen from a cup, you can sip it through a thin straw. Straws are especially convenient for taking mangosteen when you cannot sit up. If you have trouble swallowing, have someone give you mangosteen with an eyedropper.

If you want to sip mangosteen while at work, bring your mangosteen in a thermos. This will keep it cool and fresh.

For some people, sipping their mangosteen alleviates health problems more effectively than taking a full dose all at once, as described in the following chapter. Of course, others find that drinking a dose of mangosteen all at once is more helpful. Experiment to find out which method works best for you.

Section 1: Drinking Applications

6.

Drinking Mangosteen All at Once

"Cheers!"

WHEN TO DRINK MANGOSTEEN ALL AT ONCE:

- For pain.
- For emotional distress.
- For injuries.
- When taking the Trauma Dose (page 57).
- To alleviate hunger pangs when you are trying to lose weight.
- To help calm down when feeling intense emotions.
- To help wake up in the morning.
- To jump start the body into a healing cycle.
- To quickly raise your body's health and vitality.

HOW TO DRINK MANGOSTEEN ALL AT ONCE:

1. Prepare your dose of mangosteen as described in one of the other mangosteen procedures in this book.

2. Drink the entire dose in several large swallows, stopping only as needed to take a breath.

MORE ABOUT DRINKING MANGOSTEEN ALL AT ONCE:

Drinking mangosteen All at Once is like a "wake up call" that can give you a burst of energy. It also asks your body to focus on any disharmony that may be forefront in the moment. This could include physical, emotional, or even mental distress. Quickly drinking a healing substance, such as mangosteen, gives the body a kind of "shock" that can send it into the active phase of the healing cycle. The healing cycle consists of two phases. In the "active phase," positive changes are made. In the "rest phase," the cells incorporate the changes and the body gathers its strength for another active phase. (Interrupting Mangosteen Therapy, page 67, can also prompt a rest phase.)

When taking mangosteen for pain, try drinking it All at Once. For subsequent doses try both sipping them and drinking them All at Once, to find out which works best for you.

Section 1: Drinking Applications

7.

The Maintenance Dose #1

The everyday dose for relatively healthy people.

TAKE A MAINTENANCE DOSE WHEN:

- You are relatively healthy and have only minor health challenges or none at all.
- You want to boost your immune system and cellular health as a preventive measure against future illness.
- Another mangosteen therapy has alleviated or improved a particular condition, and now it is time to reduce your dosages to a maintenance level.
- You are between cycles of more vigorous mangosteen therapy such as the Top Dose Procedure (page 49) or the Technique for Stubborn Conditions (page 45).

HOW MUCH IS A MANGOSTEEN MAINTENANCE DOSE?

A Maintenance Dose for the average adult is one ounce of mangosteen per day. However, for the sake of economy consider starting with only half that amount (one tablespoonful). Then you can easily double your dose (by increasing it to one ounce) when your body needs it. In addition:

- Athletes may prefer to take an extra ounce each day.
- Overweight adults could take an extra tablespoonful for every 50 pounds of excess weight.
- Adults who have large frames, but who are not necessarily overweight, could try one or two ounces per day.
- Adults who weigh less than 100 pounds may only need one tablespoonful per day.
- Teenagers can take the same dose amount as adults.
- Children age 6 to 12 may need only two or three teaspoonfuls a day.
- Children under 6 may need only a teaspoonful a day as maintenance.

HOW TO TAKE THE MANGOSTEEN MAINTENANCE DOSE #1:

1. Decide how much mangosteen you should take each day using the guidelines above.

2. Gently shake an upside down bottle of mangosteen to disperse the rind and pulp. Measure your Maintenance Dose and pour it into a glass. Or, pour it directly into a one-ounce medicine cup.

3. Drink half the dose. Save the other half for later. Put the glass or medicine cup on a plate so it is less likely to tip over, then cover with plastic wrap or a lid and store it in the refrigerator.

4. Drink the second half of your Maintenance Dose about four to six hours later. Then pour some water into the glass or medicine cup and drink up any remaining mangosteen particles.

MORE ABOUT THE MAINTENANCE DOSE #1:

If you are using a glass, swirl it before drinking to distribute the mangosteen pulp and rind throughout the dose. A medicine cup is too small to swirl.

Taking your doses on an empty stomach allows you to obtain the best and the most from mangosteen's healing compounds. Take mangosteen at least fifteen minutes before a meal and at least thirty minutes after one. Taking mangosteen on a full stomach may cause indigestion in some people—depending on what kind of meal they have just eaten. Drinking a fruit beverage with certain types of food can result in a poor food combination that can cause distress.

If you are taking mangosteen for a condition of the upper digestive tract, which includes the stomach, esophagus, and throat, it is better to take it before eating or drinking anything for at least an hour. This way, mangosteen will coat these organs and address them directly.

It is better to divide your daily Maintenance Dose in half so that you take some mangosteen twice a day instead of all at one time. Spreading your doses allows your body to assimilate mangosteen's healing compounds more efficiently. I suggest pouring the entire dose and drinking only half of it, to make it easier and more convenient to take the second dose. All you have to do is open the refrigerator, take out the pre-measured dose, and drink.

A Maintenance Dose should supply enough mangosteen healing compounds to meet your body's daily needs. When you are stressed or ill, these needs will increase. Double or triple your Maintenance Dose on these occasions. (See also the Mangosteen Tonic on page 83, and the Mangosteen Sick-Day Prevention Dose on page 59, and the Procedure for Acute Conditions on page 33.)

If you are relatively healthy and taking the Maintenance Dose it isn't always necessary to measure an exact dose each day. After awhile, you will develop a style for drinking mangosteen. Some people do measure the exact amount that they want to take. Others pour into a glass an amount that seems "about right." And some just drink a few gulps a day straight from the bottle!

Section 1: Drinking Applications

8.

The Maintenance Dose #2

Here's an easy alternative to the Mangosteen Maintenance Dose #1.

**TRY THE MANGOSTEEN
MAINTENANCE DOSE #2 WHEN:**

- You have been taking the Maintenance Dose #1 and would like to try something different.
- The beneficial results you once got from the Maintenance Dose #1 are waning.
- You are on a tight budget and need to economize. (With this procedure, one bottle of mangosteen should last more than a month.)
- You enjoy the benefits of mangosteen but do not care for its tangy flavor.

**HOW TO TAKE THE
MANGOSTEEN MAINTENANCE DOSE #2:**

1. Gently shake a sealed, upside down bottle of mangosteen until the particles and pulp are completely mixed with the watery juice.

2. Measure one tablespoonful of mangosteen and pour it into a drinking glass.

3. Add four to eight ounces of water.

4. Sip this dose over a period of at least an hour. Or, drink half all at once and save the other half in the refrigerator for later that day.

MORE ABOUT THE
MANGOSTEEN MAINTENANCE DOSE #2:

Use only distilled water, spring water, purified tap water, or clean-and-untreated well water. Chlorine, fluorine, and other chemicals used to treat tap water may interfere with the body's ability to absorb and use mangosteen's healing compounds.

With about four ounces of water added, mangosteen will taste sweeter than when undiluted, as the water eases the tanginess. Adding more than four ounces weakens the flavor. Try using ice water for a refreshing drink, and also try adding a few drops of lemon juice.

This maintenance dose procedure suggests taking half the mangosteen usually suggested for a Maintenance Dose (page 23). Because of the water used in this procedure, the body should utilize mangosteen's healing compounds more effectively. Water transports healing compounds to the areas of the body that need them. It helps the cells take in the compounds they need. And it also helps the body flush toxins and wastes. Taking mangosteen in a glassful of water also gives your body mangosteen's healing compounds more consistently throughout the day, especially if you sip your doses. This provides a kind of support that may be particularly effective with some conditions. In addition, taking water with mangosteen allows its healing compounds to spread throughout the body more quickly than drinking mangosteen undiluted.

Section 1: Drinking Applications

9.

The Maintenance Dose #3

Some people get locked into the habit of taking only a certain number of ounces of mangosteen, using the same drinking procedures, every day. Such a habit can be beneficial at first, but after awhile it can make the body complacent. Then the body may not respond to mangosteen as well as it once did. This chapter shows you how your body can obtain the maximum benefit from mangosteen even years after you have added it to your diet.

**TRY THE MANGOSTEEN
MAINTENANCE DOSE #3 WHEN:**

- You are relatively healthy and have only minor health challenges or none at all.
- You have been taking the Mangosteen Maintenance Dose #1 and/or #2 for many months.
- The Maintenance Dose that you have been taking does not seem to give you the same support or health benefits as it did before.
- You have suddenly been faced with new challenges, changes or stress and your budget does not allow you to add extra ounces of mangosteen to your diet to compensate.
- You want to develop a greater degree of comfort with and confidence in taking mangosteen.

HOW TO TAKE THE
MANGOSTEEN MAINTENANCE DOSE #3:

One or two days each week:
- If you usually drink mangosteen undiluted as in Maintenance Dose #1 (page 23), try mixing it with water as in Maintenance Dose #2 (page 27).
- Likewise, if you usually drink mangosteen with water, try taking your doses undiluted.
- One or two days a week, take a different amount of mangosteen than you usually do. For example, drink three or four ounces instead of one or two. On another day, try taking less mangosteen than you usually do. For example, if you usually take one or two ounces daily, try taking just one teaspoonful.
- Try Interrupting Mangosteen Therapy (page 67).
- Sip your doses of mangosteen (page 19) instead of drinking them All at Once (page 21) or vice versa.
- Try taking your mangosteen at different times of the day. This will help you discover mangosteen's effect on your body. It will also help you find the best time of day to take mangosteen for your particular needs. (See also "Mangosteen and the Chinese Body Clock" on page 63.) Here are some ideas for various times to take mangosteen:

  - Immediately upon awakening.
  - Right before a meal.
  - During a meal.
  - After a meal.
  - Before exercise.
  - During exercise. (Sip during breaks.)
  - After exercise.
  - When you feel like taking a nap.
  - Before or after satisfying a sugar or caffeine craving.
  - Right before going to sleep at night. (If you are concerned this might keep you awake, don't try it before days when you have to wake up early and refreshed. But on those days, be sure to try a morning dose.)

In addition:
- Experiment with other ways to use mangosteen presented in this book. Every so often, try a topical or internal application that you've never done before.
- Play with the Technique for Stubborn Conditions (page 45) and vary your doses daily for a week or two every couple of months.
- Try other creative ways to take mangosteen that you might think of.
- Keep mangosteen a Family Friend (page 113).

MORE ABOUT THE MANGOSTEEN MAINTENANCE DOSE #3:

The philosophy of Maintenance Dose #3 is to pay attention to how mangosteen is helping you and don't make a habit of taking the same dose in the same way all the time. Feel free to experiment. Remember that an attitude of creativity and flexibility and a willingness to try new things makes the body more receptive to health and healing.

The Mangosteen Maintenance Dose #3 has no hard, fast rules. It is meant to remind you to be flexible with mangosteen. Change is a constant in our lives, and mangosteen will be there to help—especially if we can feel comfortable enough to modify the way we use mangosteen to meet our changing needs.

Section 1: Drinking Applications

10.

A Procedure for Acute Conditions

The suggested dosage for acute conditions is considerably higher than the maintenance dosage. But it is taken only for as long as the acute condition lasts, usually no more than two or three weeks. Acute conditions are short-lived, usually start quickly and are often relatively severe.

**TRY THIS PROCEDURE FOR
ACUTE CONDITIONS INCLUDING:**

- Back pain.
- Bladder infections.
- Bronchitis.
- Cold sores.
- Common cold.
- Cough.
- Earache.
- Fever.
- Gastrointestinal upsets.
- Infections.
- Influenza.
- Injuries.
- PMS.
- Rashes.
- Ringworm.
- Sinusitis.
- Sore throat.
- Toothache.
- Yeast infections.

HOW TO FOLLOW THE PROCEDURE FOR ACUTE CONDITIONS:

1. Take four or five ounces of mangosteen a day:

   - Each individual dose can be from one-half ounce (one tablespoonful) to one ounce.
   - Spread your doses throughout the day, but don't hesitate to take a dose when your symptoms are particularly bothersome.
   - Experiment with Sipping your doses (page 19) and drinking them All at Once (page 21).
   - Also experiment with drinking your doses undiluted or with water, to see which eases your symptoms the best.
   - Also try taking your doses in the form of Mangosteen Tea (page 75).

2. Meanwhile, use topical and internal applications of mangosteen (Sections 2 and 3 of this book), to address your symptoms directly and to support your recovery.

3. When your symptoms abate, reduce your total daily dosage by one ounce. After a few days, reduce your total daily dosage once again by one ounce. Continue to reduce your total daily dosage in this way until you have returned to your daily Maintenance Dose.

MORE ABOUT THE PROCEDURE FOR ACUTE CONDITIONS:

Acute conditions include a wide range of symptoms, locations and causes. This why Steps 1 and 2 suggest trying various ways to take mangosteen, to see what works best for you. Don't be shy about experimenting with mangosteen—or coming up with your own ways to use it.

One significant way to experiment with your doses is to drink them either undiluted or with water. When taken undiluted, mangosteen is more likely to stimulate the active phase of the healing cycle (page 22), which can be particularly helpful for acute conditions. On the other

Section 1: Drinking Applications

hand, the added water will ease any symptoms that may be the result of dehydration. Water also flushes toxins from your body which may be causing or exacerbating certain symptoms.

As your acute condition improves, it is important to reduce your total daily dosage of mangosteen slowly over several days. Then your body continues to receive the support of mangosteen's healing compounds as it completes its healing. Just because your outer symptoms may have abated or gone away does not mean that your body is completely healed or infection-free. It takes some time for your body's systems to regain their former level of vitality. Let mangosteen help you in this final phase of your acute condition too.

If you are relatively healthy and feel an acute condition coming on, try increasing your daily Maintenance Dose by one ounce. This may be enough to thwart the condition at its onset. This is also the most economical approach. However, if an acute condition starts out relatively severe, don't hesitate to take a full five ounces of mangosteen a day. Justify the cost involved with what you will probably save in time away from work, repeated doctor visits and over-the-counter remedies. Of course, if your acute condition is severe, do see your doctor.

This procedure for Acute Conditions can also be helpful for skin conditions, as it improves the body's overall immune system. Try it for acute skin conditions such as ringworm, infections, acne, wounds, dermatitis, fungus, eczema eruptions, poison ivy, insect bites, and rashes and itchiness of all kinds. Drinking mangosteen helps address these conditions from the inside, bringing to the area helpful healing compounds with antihistaminic, antiseptic, anti-fungal and anti-viral properties. For best results, apply mangosteen topically as well.

Section 1: Drinking Applications

11.

A Procedure for Chronic Conditions

The suggested dosage for chronic conditions is slightly higher than the maintenance dosage. This may be all you need to curb chronic symptoms. If you consider your chronic condition severe, or if it does not respond to the procedure in this chapter, see the Procedures for Health Improvement on pages 39 and 41. Chronic conditions are those that last for a long time or recur frequently.

TRY THIS PROCEDURE FOR CONDITIONS SUCH AS:

- Acid reflux disease.
- Allergies.
- Arthritis.
- Asthma.
- Atherosclerosis.
- Bowel Disorders.
- Bronchitis.
- Chronic fatigue.
- Colitis.
- Depression.
- Diabetes.
- Diverticulitis.
- Emphysema.
- Fibromyalgia.
- Herpes.
- High blood pressure.
- High cholesterol.
- HIV.
- Hyperactivity and ADHD.
- Hypoglycemia.
- Infection (local or internal).
- Inflammatory bowel disease.
- Itchiness.
- Multiple sclerosis.
- Pain.
- Pulmonary disease.
- Rheumatoid arthritis.
- Skin conditions.
- Yeast infection.

HOW TO FOLLOW THE
PROCEDURE FOR CHRONIC CONDITIONS:

1. Start by following the Loading Dose procedure on page 15.

2. Then take two to four one-ounce doses of mangosteen a day. For best absorption of mangosteen's healing compounds, take your doses on an empty stomach, and separate each dose by at least a few hours.

3. If your chronic condition has a localized area, use topical or internal applications as described in Sections 2 and 3 of this book.

4. After your symptoms have improved for a few weeks, Interrupt Mangosteen Therapy (page 67) for a few days. Then resume your previous dosage, or try reducing it to a Maintenance Dose.

MORE ABOUT THE
PROCEDURE FOR CHRONIC CONDITIONS:

Before pouring each dose, be sure to shake the sealed bottle of mangosteen upside down until the pulp and particles are well mixed throughout the juice.

The Procedure for Chronic Conditions is designed to promote a slow but gradual improvement in your overall health and well-being. As a result, the underlying problem can be addressed—not just the symptoms. So, plan to follow this procedure for several months, even as your symptoms get better. Chronic conditions may take a while to improve, simply because they are typically long-lasting. If you have had the condition for a long time it may be deeply rooted in your body. As uncomfortable as your symptoms may be, the body can become accustomed to them. This makes healthful change more difficult too.

As an added benefit to doing this Procedure, you may find relief from other, relatively minor conditions that you might also have. Improvement in these conditions gives you a strong indication that mangosteen is indeed helping you, even though it might take much longer to see improvements in chronic symptoms. Keep track of all your health improvements with the Health Evaluation Questionnaire in Appendix 1 (see page 227).

Section 1: Drinking Applications

12.
A Procedure for Health Improvement #1

This procedure is designed for people with conditions that they consider "serious." Serious conditions disrupt a person's ability to lead a normal lifestyle. See the Procedure for Health Improvement #2 (page 41) if your serious condition is life-threatening or has the potential to become so.

TRY THIS PROCEDURE FOR:

- Chronic conditions listed on page 37 which you consider serious.
- Conditions whose symptoms plague you daily.

**HOW TO DO THE
PROCEDURE FOR HEALTH IMPROVEMENT #1:**

1. Take four to six ounces of mangosteen a day for at least two weeks. Spread the ounces throughout the day. Take them on an empty stomach. You could take two ounces at a time.

2. When your symptoms improve, reduce your daily dosage gradually over a period of several weeks. Cut it back by only one or two tablespoonfuls each week.

MORE ABOUT THE
PROCEDURE FOR HEALTH IMPROVEMENT #1:

As you wean yourself from the higher dosage, your body should remain symptom free due to improved health. Continue to reduce your doses until you are following the Procedure for Chronic Conditions (page 37). But if your symptoms return, start again with the larger dosage suggested in this chapter. Next time, reduce your dosage more gradually.

This procedure suggests taking four to six ounces of mangosteen a day. This is similar to a Loading Dose. The difference is that you take this amount of mangosteen for a much longer period of time, until your symptoms improve.

Taking your doses on an empty stomach allows you to obtain the best and the most from mangosteen's healing compounds. Take mangosteen at least fifteen minutes before a meal and at least thirty minutes after one. It is better to spread your doses throughout the day. Doing so allows your body to assimilate mangosteen's nutrients more efficiently.

Section 1: Drinking Applications

13.

A Procedure for Health Improvement #2

This is an aggressive protocol for conditions that are very serious and potentially life-threatening. It is similar to the Procedure for Health Improvement #1 except that dosages are higher and more care needs to be taken when symptoms improve and you are tempted to reduce your total daily dosage. As with the other suggestions in this book, use this procedure in addition to the protocols your doctor recommends.

TRY THIS PROCEDURE FOR:

- Chronic conditions listed on page 37 which you consider serious.
- When your ability to enjoy life is severely impaired.
- Injuries.
- Serious conditions that are not responding to other forms of treatment.
- And when the doctors say there is nothing else they can do.

HOW TO DO THE
PROCEDURE FOR HEALTH IMPROVEMENT #2:

1. Take eight to twelve ounces of mangosteen a day. The more serious you consider your condition, the higher your daily dosage should be. Spread the ounces throughout the day. Take them on an empty stomach. You could take two ounces at a time.

2. When your symptoms improve, reduce your daily dosage by one or two ounces. Take this amount daily for at least two weeks.

3. If your symptoms continue to improve, reduce your daily dosage by another ounce or two. Take this amount for a few weeks.

4. Continue to reduce your daily dosage by one or two ounces every few weeks until you reach a daily dosage of two to four ounces. (See the Procedure for Chronic Conditions on page 37.) Continue to take this amount daily. If your symptoms return, repeat the Procedure for Health Improvement #2 starting with Step 1. This sudden increase in your daily dosage may curb deteriorating symptoms at the onset.

MORE ABOUT THE
PROCEDURE FOR HEALTH IMPROVEMENT #2:

For variety, try adding water to some of your doses. Try Sipping (page 19) and drinking them All at Once (page 21). Also try Mangosteen Tea. If you have trouble drinking this many ounces of mangosteen a day, also try adding it to foods (page 97).

If you are too weak to drink or sip mangosteen juice, have someone give you drops of the juice with an eyedropper or spoon, as often as every few minutes.

When your symptoms improve, it is important to reduce your daily dosages slowly. However, this can be very difficult and requires extraordinary self-discipline. After all, you are feeling better so why bother taking so much mangosteen? Over the years, I have observed an interesting but unfortunate pattern. People with serious conditions who reduce their dosages of a natural healing substance too quickly may find

Section 1: Drinking Applications

not only that their symptoms return, but that their body does not respond to the healing substance as effectively as it did before. Reducing a dosage gradually is essential to give the body time to heal. Just because symptoms abate doesn't mean that the underlying condition is healed. This can take time, and during that time, mangosteen's support can be invaluable.

This procedure involves a considerable amount of mangosteen. Be sure to have enough on hand so you won't run out. If taking this much mangosteen makes you feel better, but then your supply runs out, your progress may be seriously set back. Interrupting Mangosteen Therapy (page 67), either intentionally or due to lack of mangosteen, is not suggested for seriously ill people until after they have felt considerably better for several months.

Section 1: Drinking Applications

14.

A Technique for Stubborn Conditions

This procedure involves varying your daily dose of mangosteen in order to challenge your cells with change and stimulate them toward greater health. Use it to schedule Maintenance Doses as well as the doses recommended in the Procedures for Acute and Chronic Conditions. If you are following a Procedure for Health Improvement, your body probably needs a steady and consistent supply of mangosteen to help heal and repair the body and supply it with needed nourishment. In this case, try this procedure only if mangosteen doesn't seem to be helping your serious condition.

TRY THIS TECHNIQUE WHEN:

- You are looking to add variety to your daily doses of mangosteen.
- Certain symptoms improve after taking mangosteen but then return.
- You have tried everything (including other mangosteen procedures) and a condition stubbornly won't get better.
- You have taken mangosteen daily for a month or two and have not achieved satisfactory results with a particular condition.
- It seems you have reached a healing plateau and cannot seem to improve beyond it.

HOW TO DO THE
TECHNIQUE FOR STUBBORN CONDITIONS:

1. Calculate how many ounces of mangosteen you usually take each week. To do this, simply multiply your daily dosage by seven.

   For example, if you usually drink two ounces of mangosteen a day, then you usually take fourteen ounces a week. (Two ounces times seven days in a week equals fourteen.)

   Note: When following this technique, you will continue to take the same number of ounces of mangosteen per week. But you will vary the number of ounces that you take each day.

2. Plan ahead how many ounces of mangosteen you will take each day for the next week. (See the examples on the following pages.) Write on a calendar the number of ounces you plan to take each day. Try to vary the doses as much as possible from day to day:

   - Schedule the same dose of mangosteen for no more than two days in a row.
   - One day each week, plan to take zero ounces of mangosteen. This would give you some of the benefits of Interrupting Mangosteen Therapy (page 67). If you usually take only one ounce of mangosteen per day, you will have to schedule these "zero days" several times a week.
   - Another day each week, plan to take six to eight ounces of mangosteen. If you usually take only one or two ounces a day, this may mean increasing your weekly allotment of mangosteen. But it can be worthwhile to experiment and see for yourself the effects of taking an extra amount of mangosteen on one day.

3. Check your plan by adding up the number of ounces you have written down for each seven-day period. They should add up to the weekly amount you calculated in Step 1.

4. Every day, refer to your calendar to find out how many ounces of mangosteen you plan to take that day. Spread the doses throughout the day.

Note: The daily doses given in the following two examples are suggestions only. There are almost limitless scheduling possibilities.

EXAMPLE #1:

Step 1: Let's say you usually take one ounce of mangosteen a day. Multiply one ounce times seven days per week, and you find that you usually take seven ounces of mangosteen a week.

Step 2: Your proposed weekly schedule could then be:
- 1 ounce on Monday
- 0 ounces on Tuesday
- 2 ounces on Wednesday
- 3 ounce on Thursday
- 0 ounces on Friday
- 0 ounce on Saturday
- 1 ounces on Sunday

7 ounces total

Step 3: In checking your plan, you find that these daily amounts total seven ounces.

EXAMPLE #2:

Step 1: Let's say you usually take two ounces of mangosteen a day. Multiply two ounces times seven days per week, and you find that you usually take fourteen ounces of mangosteen a week.

Step 2: Your proposed weekly schedule could then be:
- 1 ounce on Monday
- 4 ounces on Tuesday
- 2 ounces on Wednesday
- 1 ounce on Thursday
- 3 ounces on Friday
- 1 ounce on Saturday
- 2 ounces on Sunday

14 ounces total

Step 3: In checking your plan, you find that these daily amounts total fourteen ounces.

EXAMPLE #3:

Step 1: Let's say you usually take three ounces of mangosteen a day. Multiply three times seven days per week, and you find that you usually take twenty-one ounces of mangosteen a week.

Step 2: Your proposed weekly schedule might then be:

    3 ounce on Monday
    0 ounces on Tuesday
    5 ounces on Wednesday
    2 ounces on Thursday
    1 ounce on Friday
    8 ounces on Saturday
    2 ounces on Sunday
    21 ounces total

Step 3: In checking your plan, you find that these daily amounts total twenty-one ounces.

MORE ABOUT THE
TECHNIQUE FOR STUBBORN CONDITIONS:

Try this technique for three or four weeks. If it is helping, continue to take mangosteen in this way.

The Technique for Stubborn Conditions is based on the principle that our cells will become complacent if they are not challenged or stimulated. Complacent cells gradually become less healthy and vital. On the other hand, change keeps our bodies alert. Alert cells, by nature, grow healthier. Varying the doses of mangosteen that you take each day is one way to provide your cells with an environment of change. This can challenge your cells and stimulate them toward greater health.

15.

The Top Dose Procedure

Here is another way to find out how much mangosteen your body needs in order to make significant improvements in your health. This procedure can be helpful for people at all levels of health, except if you have an acute condition and need relatively large amounts of mangosteen right away. (See the Procedure for Acute Conditions on page 33.)

THE TOP DOSE PROCEDURE CAN BE HELPFUL FOR:

- Relatively healthy individuals who would like to improve their immune system and clear toxins in order to reach a new level of health.
- Those with chronic conditions who are not sure how much mangosteen their body needs in order to improve symptoms.
- Athletes who want to see if mangosteen can:
  - Enhance their performance.
  - Fine-tune their body.
  - Increase strength, stamina and endurance.
- Health-care professionals who want to evaluate the potential of mangosteen personally before offering it to patients.
- Individuals with serious conditions who are unable to afford the amount of mangosteen suggested in the Procedures for Health Improvement on pages 39 and 41. The Top Dose procedure can help them find the minimum amount of mangosteen they need for maximum results.

HOW TO DO THE TOP DOSE PROCEDURE:

Before you begin, fill out a copy of the Health Evaluation Questionnaire in Appendix 1 (page 227). This will help you spot health improvements that might otherwise go unnoticed.

Plan to keep track of how much mangosteen you take each day by marking the amount on a calendar. Also, each day record how you feel and any changes in your health—even minor ones. This way, you can look back to see how much mangosteen you were taking when these improvements occurred. It will also help you identify your Top Dose.

How to Identify your Top Dose:

1. Starting today, take one ounce of mangosteen each day for three days.

2. For the next three days take two ounces of mangosteen a day.

3. Every three days, increase your total daily dosage by either one tablespoonful (one-half ounce) or one ounce.

Stop increasing your total daily dosage when:
- A symptom that has been bothering you starts to improve.
- Your general sense of well-being or mental clarity improves.
- Your physical performance reaches a new plateau.
- You have symptoms of a possible cleansing reaction (page 233).
- You intuitively sense that you've increased your dosage enough.

This is your Top Dose.

If you sense that you are taking more mangosteen than your body can handle, or if you think you've increased your dosage too much or if you have a cleansing reaction, go back to the dose you were taking before you last increased it. This will be your Top Dose.

Section 1: Drinking Applications

What to do When you've Found your Top Dose:

1. Continue to take your Top Dose daily for a week or two.

2. Fill out another copy of the Health Evaluation Questionnaire (pages 230-231). Compare it with the copy you filled out when you began this procedure. The results will help you evaluate your health progress, the benefits of this procedure, how well this procedure worked for you and if you should repeat the procedure or try a different one.

3. Then Interrupt Mangosteen Therapy (page 67) for a few days.

4. Repeat the Top Dose Procedure, starting with Step 1, when you are ready for another cycle of active health improvement.

MORE ABOUT THE TOP DOSE PROCEDURE:

The first time you do this procedure, your Top Dose may be as little as two or three ounces a day, or it may be as much as eight to twelve ounces a day. If your Top Dose is large, your body could have a great need for mangosteen's healing compounds. However, the next time you do this procedure, your Top Dose may be different as your body's needs can change. This is why you should re-identify your Top Dose each time you do this procedure.

Also, you can start the Top Dose Procedure with one tablespoonful of mangosteen instead of the one-ounce daily dose suggested in Step 1 on page 50. Then increase your dose by just one tablespoonful each three-day period.

One way to take mangosteen is to continually repeat the Top Dose Procedure. Or, you could do this procedure for health maintenance, for example twice a year, once in Spring and once in Autumn. This would support the body's natural cleansing cycles during these seasons.

If you are doing the Top Dose Procedure to evaluate mangosteen's healing potential, also experiment with the topical and internal applications of mangosteen described in Sections 2 and 3 of this book.

Section 1: Drinking Applications

16.

The Anti-Stress Procedure

The mangosteen Anti-Stress Procedure includes many elements of good health, including relaxation, deep breathing, meditation, creative visualization, "letting go," exercising gratitude and drinking mangosteen. Together, they elevate the "plain old daily dose" into a powerful healing regimen.

**TRY THE MANGOSTEEN
ANTI-STRESS PROCEDURE WHEN:**

- You are suddenly faced with unusual stress.
- Or, you have been experiencing ongoing stress and need to relax before the effects of the stress damage your health.
- You have been taking a mangosteen Maintenance Dose for awhile and would like a stronger effect without necessarily having to take more mangosteen.
- You would like to receive a greater benefit from any procedure for taking mangosteen that you may be following (including the Procedures for Acute and Chronic Conditions, as well as the Health Improvement Procedures and others).
- You would like to try a new approach to using mangosteen for health maintenance and improvement.

HOW TO FOLLOW THE
MANGOSTEEN ANTI-STRESS PROCEDURE:

Find ten minutes in your daily schedule when you can routinely take your mangosteen. Ideally, it should be at the same time every day and at a time when the house is quiet and you can be alone. If you cannot fit an extra ten minutes into your daily routine, then grab whatever time you can spare.

1. Make a dose of Mangosteen Tea (page 75).

2. Find a comfortable place to sit and bring your cup of mangosteen with you.

3. Close your eyes, relax and take three long, deep breaths. Let your worries slip away on each exhale. Breathe in new life and vitality on each inhale. Try to visualize stress and tension leaving your body when you exhale and youthful energy entering your body on the inhale.

4. Open your eyes and take a sip of mangosteen. Hold the sip in your mouth and swallow when you need to. Take your time and try not to hurry. While holding the sip in your mouth, nurture a feeling of sincere appreciation for your body, for your health and for the circumstances that lead you to finding mangosteen.

5. Repeat Steps 3 and 4 until your dose is finished.

MORE ABOUT THE
MANGOSTEEN ANTI-STRESS PROCEDURE:

Nurturing gratitude and love for oneself and one's body, as suggested in Step 4, is another powerful way to rejuvenate and reduce stress. Try to give attention to each part of your body and feel grateful for it. If certain parts are not working as they should, send them healing energy by feeling love and appreciation for them. This technique can be magnified if you also touch or gently massage the areas of your body as you give them your attention.

Section 1: Drinking Applications

The method for taking mangosteen outlined in this chapter can be used along with any other procedure for taking mangosteen. It may be especially helpful for those with serious conditions or ailments where the organs involved can be pinpointed. Then, in Step 4, you can focus love and gratitude on that particular organ.

If you usually take mangosteen more than once a day, follow this procedure with one dose and take the other dose as you normally would. Of course, if you have the time and the desire, you can do this procedure with more than one dose per day.

At the very least, if you do not have time to follow all the steps in this procedure, at least take a few deep breaths before drinking each of your mangosteen doses and practice feeling gratitude with each one.

Breathing deeply before taking healthful supplements like mangosteen opens pathways for healing compounds to reach more cells and more deeply into the cells than with regular breathing. The extra oxygen brought into the body may also enhance the effects of that supplement.

17.

The Trauma Dose

The Trauma Dose offers a surge of healing compounds to help the body cope with extreme physical or emotional experiences.

USE THE TRAUMA DOSE FOR:

- Accidents and injuries.
- Any sudden and traumatic experience.
- Easing withdrawal symptoms.
- Emotional trauma, such as grief, sadness or anger.
- Helping the body recover after surgery.
- Sudden muscle spasms and cramps.

Note: Offer a Trauma Dose as soon as possible after First Aid has been applied and you have attended to the victim's immediate needs. However, give mangosteen orally only if the individual is awake, able to drink and not in shock.

HOW TO TAKE A TRAUMA DOSE:

1. Turn a seal bottle of mangosteen upside down and shake it to mix the rind particles. Do this quickly if time is of the essence.

2. Measure three or four ounces (one-half cup) of mangosteen and pour it into a drinking cup. Drink this All at Once (page 21).

3. Then apply a topical application appropriate for the condition, such as a Mangosteen Poultice (page 179). See Section 2, Topical Applications of Mangosteen, for other possible treatments.

4. Take a second Trauma Dose anywhere from one-half hour to several hours later. The more intense your trauma or pain, the sooner you may want to take a second dose.

5. Take a third Trauma Dose per the instructions in Step 4.

6. Then follow the Procedure for Acute Conditions (page 33).

MORE ABOUT THE TRAUMA DOSE:

Depending on the nature of the trauma, you could take several Trauma Doses within a twenty-four hour period. On the other hand, you may need only one Trauma Dose.

Ideally, the Trauma Dose should be taken all at once. Then it serves as a wake-up call that can send the body into an active phase of the healing cycle (page 22). Ideally, it will also counteract some of the effects of the trauma, thus reducing its negative impact on the body. However, if you are unable to drink the entire Trauma Dose or have trouble swallowing, sip as much as you can as often as possible. One option is to take a tablespoonful about every half-hour or hour. Another option is to sip the Trauma Dose following the instructions for the Auto-Distribution Dose (page 201).

A Trauma Dose can help reduce pain and inflammation, and help you feel more calm, restful and at ease. Tattered emotions may be soothed and healing and cell regeneration accelerated.

Some people might find it hard to drink so much cold mangosteen juice all at once if it comes straight from the refrigerator. You won't have time to warm the first Trauma Dose, but the following doses could be left at room temperature.

Section 1: Drinking Applications

18.

The Sick-Day Prevention Dose

This is a dose for the whole family. Take it in addition to your regular daily doses of mangosteen.

TRY THE MANGOSTEEN
SICK-DAY PREVENTION DOSE WHEN:

- Someone in your family has been exposed to a contagious illness.
- Someone in your family shows the first signs or symptoms of the flu or other acute illness.
- Your children seem more tired and cranky than usual. (This can be a sign of a weakened or stressed immune system, which is a precursor to illness.)
- You sense that someone in your family may be "coming down with something." You may not have any physical evidence to support this suspicion, but parents should trust their intuition. It can only help to drink extra mangosteen, just in case.

HOW TO USE MANGOSTEEN
TO PREVENT SICK DAYS:

1. Immediately give a Sick-Day Prevention Dose to the family member who is showing signs of illness. Also give one to everyone else in the family. Ideally, this dose should be taken All at Once (page 21).

2. Later that day, family members should take a second Sick-Day Prevention Dose.

3. Continue to have everyone in the family take two or three Sick-Day Prevention Doses per day for a few days, or until everyone in the family is feeling better.

HOW MUCH IS A
SICK-DAY PREVENTION DOSE?

- For adults and teenagers, two ounces.
- For preteens, one or two ounces.
- For children, one ounce.
- And for babies and toddlers, one-half ounce (one tablespoonful.)

MORE ABOUT USING
MANGOSTEEN TO PREVENT SICK DAYS:

The immune support and anti-bacterial, anti-viral and anti-fungal properties that mangosteen can provide should boost the immune system of everyone in the family and clear up infection before it spreads throughout the family. It should also reduce the potential severity of the sickness.

Sometimes children who are ill or fighting illness intuitively know that mangosteen can help them and will ask for more. Feel free to give them as much as they want, within reasonable limits (perhaps about one-half cup per dose). When the illness is passed, however, they should return to a Maintenance Dose (page 23).

The Sick-Day Prevention Dose should be taken in addition to your regular daily dosage of mangosteen.

Section 1: Drinking Applications

19.

Taking Mangosteen with Herbs and Supplements

A reminder about something that may seem obvious.

TAKE MANGOSTEEN WITH OTHER SUPPLEMENTS:

- As part of your daily routine.
- To get the maximum benefit from all your supplements.

HOW TO TAKE MANGOSTEEN WITH OTHER SUPPLEMENTS:

1. Gather the supplements you want to take. These can include vitamins, minerals, herbs and anti-oxidants. Also fill a glass with purified water, to help you take these supplements.

2. Gently shake a sealed bottle of mangosteen upside down until the rind particles are well mixed throughout the juice. Pour a dose into a medicine cup.

3. Drink your dose of mangosteen.

4. Immediately afterwards take the supplements.

MORE ABOUT TAKING MANGOSTEEN WITH OTHER SUPPLEMENTS:

Pour your mangosteen after you have gathered your supplements. Then the rind particles will have less time to fall to the bottom of the cup and it will be easier to drink them up.

Take your supplements after your drink your mangosteen. Then the water that you drink will wash the rind particles from your mouth.

Get into the routine of taking mangosteen with your other supplements, and you will be less likely to forget to take either of them. I believe that most supplements have a synergistic effect. They help each other to be absorbed into the body, and then they help each other work for the body's benefit. Increase your absorption of these nutrients even more by spreading your doses of mangosteen and other supplements throughout the day.

Take mangosteen at least fifteen minutes before taking a homeopathic remedy and at least thirty minutes afterwards. Homeopathic remedies work best on their own, by themselves.

Also try adding mangosteen to herbal teas, herbal preparations, poultices and baths. (For example, see Mangosteen Tea on page 75 and the Mangosteen Sitz Bath on page 189.) Use your judgment about how much mangosteen to add to herbs based on the quantity of herbs used and how you are going to use them. Add as much as two to six ounces of mangosteen to herbal baths. Dried mangosteen particles can also be added to dried herbal preparations and combinations.

TAKING MANGOSTEEN WITH PRESCRIPTION MEDICATIONS:

You should be able to take mangosteen along with prescription medications without problem. After all, mangosteen is simply a fruit juice. However, if you or your doctor are at all concerned about it, start with the Procedure for Gradually Introducing Mangosteen to Your Diet (page 11). Your confidence and comfort taking mangosteen should increase with each dose that you take, especially if you start to feel better.

Section 1: Drinking Applications

20.

The Mangosteen Chinese Body Clock Procedure

Centuries ago, the Chinese discovered that the body is sustained and maintained by an energy they call "chi." They found that chi is absorbed into the body at "acupuncture points." It is then spread throughout the body via channels called "acupuncture meridians."

The Chinese also discovered that chi moves through the meridians in cycles that follow a clock-like pattern. Each meridian has a two-hour segment in which its chi is the strongest. It is believed that this is the best time to treat the organs associated with that meridian. The following method for taking mangosteen reflects these ancient Chinese principles.*

TRY THE CHINESE BODY CLOCK PROCEDURE WHEN:

- You would like your doses of mangosteen to focus on a particular organ or organ system.
- You have the self-discipline to take mangosteen the same time each day, even if it means taking it in the middle of the night.
- You would like to try yet another way to obtain the most benefit from mangosteen.
- Your body (or your budget) can handle only a certain amount of mangosteen each day, but your health condition warrants taking more.
- Your health condition involves organs listed on the chart on the following page.

---

* Gerber, Richard, M.D., *Vibrational Medicine*, (Santa Fe, NM: Bear & Company), 1998, pp. 182, 183.

HOW TO DO THE
MANGOSTEEN CHINESE BODY CLOCK PROCEDURE:
METHOD 1:

1. Study the Body Clock chart on the following page, which lists the times when certain organs and their meridians receive the most chi energy.

2. Find out if the organ for which you would like to take mangosteen is present on this chart. If so, take your full daily dosage of mangosteen during the time period associated with that organ.

METHOD 2:

1. Decide which two or three organs listed on the Chinese Body Clock chart are most responsible for your health condition. You may need to ask your health-care provider for his or her input on this question. Although it may seem that we have just one ailing organ, weaknesses in other organs usually exacerbate our primary condition.

2. Refer to the Body Clock chart. Write down which time periods correspond to the organs you chose in Step 1.

3. Take a dose of mangosteen during each of these time periods.

Examples:
- Let's say you have learned that a heart condition is complicated by congested lungs. Divide your total daily dosage of mangosteen into two doses. Plan to take one at mid-day between 11:00AM and 1:00PM for the heart, and one very late at night between 3:00AM and 5:00AM for the lungs.

- Or, you may have two separate conditions you want to work on, such as a bladder infection and chronic indigestion. In this case, take your mangosteen doses during the time periods that correspond to these organs: between 3:00PM and 5:00PM for the bladder, and between 7:00AM and 9:00AM for the stomach.

- If your problem organs have adjacent time periods, such as the gall bladder (11:00PM – 1:00AM) and the liver (1:00AM – 3:00AM), you could take your dose of mangosteen on the cusp between the two. In this case, at 1:00AM.

The Chinese Body Clock

ORGAN	TIME PERIOD
Small Intestine	1:00PM – 3:00PM
Bladder	3:00PM – 5:00PM
Kidney/Adrenals	5:00PM – 7:00PM
Circulation/Sex	7:00PM – 9:00PM
Triple Warmer	9:00PM – 11:00PM
Gall Bladder	11:00PM – 1:00AM
Liver	1:00AM – 3:00AM
Lung	3:00AM – 5:00AM
Large Intestine	5:00AM – 7:00AM
Stomach	7:00AM – 9:00AM
Spleen/Pancreas/Immune System	9:00AM – 11:00AM
Heart	11:00AM – 1:00PM

MORE ABOUT THE MANGOSTEEN CHINESE BODY CLOCK PROCEDURE:

This procedure marries certain Chinese Medicine principles with taking mangosteen. Those who try this procedure may find that their body needs less mangosteen overall, and that the mangosteen they do take gives them better and more lasting results. This is because taking healthful supplements like mangosteen at certain times of the day can more strongly affect certain organs.

So before you begin this procedure, plan to reduce the total daily dosage of mangosteen that you have already been taking. For example, if you usually take three ounces a day, try taking only two. If you are following Method 2 and have chosen two organs, take one ounce for each organ. If you usually take two ounces a day and have chosen three organs to work on, try taking one-half ounce during each of the three time periods. Do not cut your total daily dosage by more than one-half, especially if mangosteen has been supporting a weakened condition. Pulling the support too quickly can needlessly stress your body's systems.

What if the organ you want to work on has a corresponding time period late at night when you are usually fast asleep, and waking up is difficult and if you do wake up, falling back to sleep is even harder? In this case, this procedure may not be the best one for you. But consider giving it a try, at least for a few nights, to see how well it works for you. Set your alarm or make an agreement with yourself to wake up (perhaps to go to the bathroom), during that time. Sometimes breaking a habit, routine or concept (in this case about sleep patterns), loosens our mindset enough to accept change, which can include healing.

If you find you are unable to take a dose of mangosteen in the middle of the night, the second best thing to do is to take a dose during the time period twelve hours away. It also helps to take your doses at exactly the same time each day.

The "triple warmer system" on the Chinese Body Clock chart may be unfamiliar to you. The triple warmer regulates the body's fluids, temperature, and energy through respiration, digestion and excretion.

There is another reason that taking supplements according to the Chinese Body Clock can be effective. Each time you take a dose at a certain time you are knowingly taking it for a particular condition and are probably also thinking about how that dose will improve the condition. This is using intention, which can be a very powerful tool no matter what therapy you are doing. Simply, each time you take a dose of mangosteen, remind yourself that the dose is going to help your body heal a specific condition.

21.
Interrupting Mangosteen Therapy

Mangosteen can be a life-long friend. But every so often it can be beneficial to stop taking mangosteen for short periods of time. Then, once you start taking mangosteen again, you may feel better than you did before.

TRY INTERRUPTING MANGOSTEEN THERAPY WHEN:

- Conditions that mangosteen once alleviated return.
- Your health has improved to a plateau and doesn't seem to be getting any better.
- You have been using mangosteen daily for awhile and now it is time to give your body a rest in order to honor natural healing cycles.
- You want to avoid letting your body become accustomed to mangosteen, so that you don't have to keep increasing your doses to get the same results.
- You want to evaluate how well mangosteen is working for you by comparing your condition when taking, then not taking, and then taking mangosteen once again.
- You want to encourage your cells to use mangosteen's healing compounds more effectively and efficiently.

HOW TO INTERRUPT MANGOSTEEN THERAPY:

1. Take daily doses of mangosteen for at least two or three months.

2. Then stop taking mangosteen for two to seven days.

3. Start taking mangosteen again, only this time try lowering your dosage.

MORE ABOUT INTERRUPTING MANGOSTEEN THERAPY:

If you are relatively healthy, Interrupt Mangosteen Therapy for about a week, every two months. This will keep your body as receptive to mangosteen's healing compounds as possible and maximize your body's utilization of them. In general, those with health challenges might stop taking mangosteen for only two or three days every two or three months. When deciding how long to Interrupt Mangosteen Therapy, consider how serious your health challenges are. The more serious, the less often you should Interrupt Mangosteen Therapy and for shorter periods of time.

Do not Interrupt Mangosteen Therapy if mangosteen has been helping to ease serious symptoms, or if you have immune deficiency conditions, diabetes or cancer. These conditions require constant support.

- If you have serious symptoms which mangosteen is helping to relieve, be careful Interrupting Mangosteen Therapy. Certainly, if your symptoms return while following this procedure, start again on mangosteen immediately. Also, be sure to alert your physician.
- In the case of immune deficiency conditions, the body requires a course of steady support for gradual improvement. Withdrawing mangosteen's support may cause the immune system to lose too much ground on its progress toward greater health.
- With diabetes, the body requires stable blood sugar levels. Withdrawing mangosteen could cause unnecessary swings in the body's chemistry.
- To fight cancer, the body needs constant and aggressive therapy. Withdrawing mangosteen after it has helped to improve your condition is like asking your armies to retreat before the battle is completely won.

Section 1: Drinking Applications

If mangosteen doesn't seem to be helping auto-immune conditions (those in which the immune system attacks certain cells as if they were foreign), try Interrupting Mangosteen Therapy for one day every one or two weeks. This is another way to urge the body into a healing cycle.

The healing cycle consists of alternating phases of rest followed by phases in which healing changes take place. Both parts of the cycle are essential to make lasting improvements in the body's health. Interrupting Mangosteen Therapy tends to initiate the rest phase of this cycle. Reintroducing mangosteen back into the diet can jumpstart the body into the phase where it makes positive change.

Removing mangosteen temporarily from the diet may also prompt the cells to recognize that they cannot rely on a steady supply of mangosteen healing compounds. They cannot take the presence of these compounds for granted. When mangosteen is reintroduced, the cells may better appreciate these healing compounds and use them more effectively and efficiently.

If you have been taking mangosteen for awhile and symptoms it once alleviated return, it is tempting to take larger doses of mangosteen to maintain the same results. Taking larger doses may indeed help. But if symptoms again return, consider Interrupting Mangosteen Therapy. In this case, the procedure may readjust the body's relationship with mangosteen's healing compounds. It can encourage the cells to use these compounds more effectively and efficiently. Then, smaller and/or previous dosages may become helpful once again.

22.
Locating Mangosteen's Healing Target

Healthful substances like mangosteen rarely work on the entire body at once. Rather, areas of greatest need or priority are targeted first. Knowing where these areas are provides invaluable information about your body as well as how to proceed on your healing journey.

This technique is based on the fact that healing substances, such as mangosteen, not only have phytoceutical healing compounds measurable in a laboratory, but also a non-measurable but often palpable and identifiable "healing energy." This healing energy starts working on the body almost immediately after a healing substance is placed in the mouth (or when applied topically). The healing energy of a powerful therapeutic substance such as mangosteen can be strong enough to feel, even by the average individual with no apparent abilities to sense such things. Some people can even visually perceive where the mangosteen healing energy is going when they look at someone who is holding mangosteen in their mouth, or who has recently taken a dose.

USE THIS PROCEDURE TO:

- Find out where in your body mangosteen might be working first.
- Locate areas of your body most in need of therapeutic attention.
- Develop your personal level of body awareness and sensitivity.
- Allow your body to tell you how much mangosteen it needs per dose.

HOW TO LOCATE MANGOSTEEN'S HEALING TARGET:

1. Pour a dose of mangosteen.

2. Take a large sip and hold it in your mouth for the entire procedure.

3. Close your eyes. Take a deep breath to relax and tune into yourself.

4. With your attention, scan your entire body. Do you sense warmth or tingling anywhere? Can you tell if mangosteen's healing energy is collecting or targeting someplace in your body? If you have areas of pain, try to sense any improvement. Try to notice any areas of your body relaxing or letting go of tension. Also trust your intuitive sense of "knowing" where the healing energy is pooling and where positive change is taking place. This will be mangosteen's healing target.

5. Continue this technique for about twenty to thirty seconds. In the meantime, swallow if you have to, but try to keep as much mangosteen in your mouth as possible.

Note: Try not to pay attention to the taste or the sensation of mangosteen's presence in your mouth. Do your best to tune into other parts of your body. If the taste is too distracting, dilute the mangosteen with some water and try again.

Section 1: Drinking Applications

MORE ABOUT LOCATING MANGOSTEEN'S HEALING TARGET:

When you are finished with the technique, swallow the mangosteen. However, spit out the mangosteen if you have problems with mercury poisoning in your mouth, cancer in your head or mouth, or a serious infection there. In these cases, the mangosteen that you hold in your mouth can absorb toxins, which you shouldn't swallow. (See the Oral Detox on page 213.) You can also tell if the mangosteen has absorbed toxins if its flavor becomes unpleasant while you are holding it in your mouth. In any case, the flavor will change somewhat even in the relatively healthy person, but it won't be unpleasant. It may become more mild, sweeter or less tangy, depending on your body's chemistry.

This technique for Locating Mangosteen's Healing Target teaches body awareness and sensitivity. These skills are invaluable for they can also help you evaluate other nutritional supplements and even foods.

Practice the technique with at least one sip from each dose of mangosteen that you take each day. This technique can be used with any procedure for drinking mangosteen in this book. It may be most apparent, however, when taking your first dose for the same reasons that it is easier to evaluate the immediate effects of mangosteen with a first dose (see page 7).

This technique is also effective for helping you decide exactly how much mangosteen your body needs. If you try this technique with one sip after another, you may find that at some point, perhaps even before your dose is finished, that you are taking smaller and smaller sips, and eventually it can seem as though you just can't take another sip. You body feels so "full" that it can't hold any more. This occurs because when you tune into mangosteen's healing energy, you become more consciously aware of what your body really needs. And your body, in turn, will tell you.

The reason I urge people to practice and find success with this technique is the wealth of information that you can gain from it. For example, one time when doing this technique, I noticed a tingling sensation in my wrists and forearms. At the time, I had a relatively serious health condition that had nothing to do with my wrists and forearms. So why would mangosteen's energies pool there? I soon realized that I had been resting my wrists and forearms on the edge of my laptop computer and likely, the electromagnetic radiation (EMR) from the laptop's strong battery was draining the vitality from those areas of my body. The mangosteen healing energy was pooling there to counteract the negative effects of the EMR. As a result of this experience, I installed a separate keyboard, which keeps my body farther away from the EMR source. This of course, allowed mangosteen's healing energy to then address other health issues.

Section 1: Drinking Applications

23.

Mangosteen Tea

Adding hot water to mangosteen should not hurt mangosteen's healing compounds. In fact, I believe the body absorbs these compounds more readily when you drink mangosteen at a warm temperature.

TRY MANGOSTEEN TEA:

- In place of your regular doses of mangosteen, or in addition to them when you need immune system support.
- At the onset of flu-like symptoms. (See the Sick-Day Prevention Dose on page 59.)
- For throat conditions including sore throat, swollen glands and tonsillitis.
- To help relieve the symptoms of common cold and flu.
- As a tonic before or during flu season or times of unusual stress. (See the Mangosteen Tonic on page 83.)
- To help you relax after a stressful day. (See the Anti-Stress Procedure on page 53.)

HOW TO MAKE MANGOSTEEN TEA METHOD 1:

1. Pour one ounce of mangosteen into a teacup or mug. (Don't use plastic or paper cups, and be sure to shake the mangosteen bottle thoroughly before pouring.)

2. Boil about a cup of purified water.

3. Pour the boiling water into a one-cup glass measuring cup. This will allow you to measure how much water you want to use. It will also reduce the water temperature enough so that it shouldn't affect mangosteen's healing compounds.

4. Pour four to eight ounces of water into the cup of mangosteen. The more water you use, the weaker the tea will taste. Experiment to find your preference.

5. If you'd like, add honey to sweeten the tea.

6. Sip, as you would drink tea.

HOW TO MAKE MANGOSTEEN TEA METHOD 2:

1. Put a teabag of your choice into a teacup or mug. Use whatever kind of tea you like. If you are using mangosteen for a particular condition, you may want to select an herbal tea that can also address that condition. Black tea, caffeinated or decaffeinated, tastes particularly good when mixed with mangosteen.

2. Boil about a cup of purified water.

3. Add the water to the teacup, leaving enough room in the cup to add an ounce of mangosteen. Let the tea steep for as long as you like. Remove the teabag.

4. Before the tea cools, add one-half to one ounce of mangosteen. (Shake the mangosteen bottle thoroughly before pouring.)

5. If you'd like, add honey to sweeten the tea.

6. Sip, as you would drink tea.

HOW TO MAKE MANGOSTEEN ICED TEA
METHOD 1:

1. Measure four to eight ounces of mangosteen juice and pour into a pitcher.

2. Add about two quarts of purified water. If you want to add honey or mint leaves for flavor, use hot (but not boiling) water. When the tea is cold, try adding some lemon juice.

3. Store the pitcher in the refrigerator until cold. Serve over ice cubes.

HOW TO MAKE MANGOSTEEN ICED TEA
METHOD 2:

1. Add several teabags of your choice to a pitcher.

2. Boil about two quarts of purified water and pour the water into the pitcher.

3. When the tea has finished steeping, remove the tea bags.

4. Add two to six ounces of mangosteen.

5. If you'd like, while the tea is still hot, add honey and mint leaves for flavor. When the tea cools, try adding some lemon juice.

6. Store the pitcher in the refrigerator until cold. Serve over ice cubes.

MORE ABOUT MANGOSTEEN TEA:

To make Mangosteen Tea, use spring water, distilled water, filtered water or pure well water. Do not use chlorinated or fluoridated water. These chemicals may interfere with the body's ability to absorb mangosteen's healing compounds.

Hot Mangosteen Tea feels wonderfully soothing, especially on a sore throat. But if your Mangosteen Tea cools off, it is still beneficial to drink.

Check the temperature of Mangosteen Tea before giving it to children, to make sure it isn't too hot for them.

The mangosteen rind particles left over at the bottom of the teacup are tasteless and anticlimactic after drinking the sweet mangosteen tea. So instead of eating them after your tea is finished, wipe them up with a finger or a spoon and put them in a small lidded jar and save them in the refrigerator. Use them later in food (see "Adding Mangosteen to Recipes" on page 97.) Or make them into a Mangosteen Decoction (page 79).

Section 1: Drinking Applications

24.

A Mangosteen Decoction

A "decoction" involves extracting the flavor and healing compounds of a substance through boiling. It is stronger than a tea, which involves only steeping a substance in hot water.

TRY THE MANGOSTEEN DECOCTION FOR:

- Cystitis.
- Diarrhea.
- Gonorrhea.
- Gleet. (Inflammation of the urethra resulting from chronic gonorrhea and characterized by a mucopurulent discharge.*)
- Also try topically for eczema and other skin disorders.

HOW TO MAKE THE MANGOSTEEN DECOCTION:

1. Place a fine mesh strainer over a one-cup measuring cup.

2. Shake a sealed bottle of mangosteen upside down until the rind particles are thoroughly mixed with the rest of the juice.

3. Pour a two-ounce dose (one-quarter cup) through the strainer and into the measuring cup. (Do this immediately after you

---

* According to the American Heritage Dictionary

have shaken the bottle so that the rind particles don't have time to settle to the bottom of the bottle. This way you can obtain as much of the rind particles as possible.)

4. Pour the strained mangosteen juice into a drinking glass. Save this for drinking your next dose(s) of mangosteen. Your measuring cup will now be empty. Add one cup of purified water to the measuring cup.

5. Turn the strainer upside down over a small pot. Though some rind particles may fall into the pot, most will probably stick to the strainer. To release them into the pot, pour the cup of water slowly through the back of the strainer. If any particles remain in the strainer, tap it against the edge of the pot.

6. Bring the water-rind mixture to a boil. Then turn the burner to "low" and cover the pot. Let it boil for one hour. Over time, the water will turn a dark amber color.

7. Let the water-rind mixture cool for a few minutes, and then pour it through the strainer once again. The healing compounds in the rind particles should now be boiled out into the water, so you can throw the leftover rind away.

8. Some of the water in the pot may have boiled away, but you should have at least one-half cup of amber-colored Mangosteen Decoction left. It tastes very mild. Take one tablespoonful every hour or two, until symptoms abate. Make a fresh batch as needed.

MORE ABOUT THE MANGOSTEEN DECOCTION:

Traditionally, mangosteen is a key ingredient of a tea used to treat diarrhea plus other ailments. This procedure gives a recipe for a decoction that might be similar to that used by traditional Asian healers. The idea for this chapter came from an excerpt of a book, "Fruits of Warm Climates" by Julie F. Morton, which I found on the internet. Ms. Morton is a Research Professor of Biology, a renowned botanist, and an expert on toxic, edible and otherwise useful plants. She writes, "The rind decoction is taken to relieve diarrhea and cystitis, gonorrhea and gleet and is applied externally as an astringent lotion. A portion of the rind is steeped in water overnight and the infusion given as a remedy for chronic diarrhea in adults and children."*

Ms. Morton also mentions that the rind can be made into an ointment and applied on eczema and other skin disorders. So, try the Mangosteen Decoction as a Rash Plaster (page 183), or simply wipe a few drops on the skin.

---

* Morton, Julia F., *Fruits of Warm Climates*, (Miami, FL: Julia F. Morton), 1987, pp. 301–304. (http://www.hort.purdue.edu/newcrop/morton/mangosteen.html)

Section 1: Drinking Applications

25.

The Mangosteen Tonic

The Mangosteen Tonic can help your body handle stressful situations by giving your immune system an added boost.

TAKE A MANGOSTEEN TONIC BEFORE POTENTIALLY STRESSFUL SITUATIONS SUCH AS:

- Birthdays, holidays or anytime you plan to eat greater quantities of food or more sugar, fat and refined foods than usual.
- Domestic upheavals, from family squabbles to divorce.
- Events that may be particularly stressful, such as exams, presentations, speeches and competitions.
- Recitals and other on-stage performances.
- Surgery.
- The beginning of school (or day care for young children).
- Traveling, especially out of the country.
- Visits to the doctor's, dentist's or attorney's office.

HOW TO TAKE A MANGOSTEEN TONIC:

1. Prepare your immune system and nervous system in the days and weeks prior to the upcoming stressful situation by taking two or three doses a day of Mangosteen Tonic, in addition to your regular daily Maintenance Dose.

2. For isolated events, take extra doses of mangosteen on the day of the event. Take a dose immediately before the event begins and another as soon as possible afterwards.

3. If the event lasts more than a day, continue to take the Mangosteen Tonic until the event ends. Then return to your usual dosage.

HOW MUCH IS A MANGOSTEEN TONIC?

- For adults and teenagers, try a dose of one ounce.
- For children, try one tablespoonful.
- For toddlers and babies, try one or two teaspoonfuls.

MORE ABOUT THE MANGOSTEEN TONIC:

Feel free to modify the amount of each dose and how many doses you take per day. Do so by evaluating how severe the stressful situation is and how strongly it affects you or your children. Also, trust your intuition and common sense about how much mangosteen to take. This is one of the benefits of using an all-natural therapeutic juice such as mangosteen. Whereas one must not adjust pharmaceutical medications without the advice of a physician, individuals are free to modify their mangosteen doses based on their own common sense.

26.

The Mangosteen Fast #1

During this fast, your entire diet will consist of mangosteen juice.

USE THE MANGOSTEEN FAST METHOD #1 IF YOU:

- Are relatively healthy.
- Are accustomed to fasting.
- Enjoy fasting for general health maintenance.
- Would like the benefits of fasting which include detoxification, improved mental clarity and greater health and well-being.
- Suspect that your body may harbor parasites and would like to use mangosteen to create a healthy environment in your body which would expel them.
- Would like to correct bad eating habits.

HOW TO DO THE MANGOSTEEN FAST METHOD #1:

1. During this fast, replace all the food and liquid in your diet with mangosteen. Drink approximately six to twelve one-ounce doses of mangosteen each day. During this fast, vary the amount of water that you take with each dose.

    - Take some doses undiluted.
    - Try some doses with approximately two, four, six and eight

ounces of water to see which dilution you enjoy the most.
- Take some doses in the form of hot Mangosteen Tea or Mangosteen Iced Tea.
- Keep yourself hydrated by drinking at least eight to ten glassfuls of water a day. Include some mangosteen in each glassful.
- Try one-half to one ounce of your daily dosage of mangosteen in each glassful.
- Or, add one ounce of mangosteen to a pitcher of water and drink freely from it throughout the day.

2. Spread the doses throughout the day, but drink some whenever you feel hungry.

3. Transition back to a "normal" diet with the following in mind:

- Give yourself a few days to make this transition.
- Continue to drink at least eight to ten glassfuls of water a day.
- Introduce other beverages back into your diet slowly and in small amounts.
- Gradually introduce foods back into your diet. Start with small meals that consist of foods that are easily digestible, such as fresh fruit and cooked vegetables. Then add whole grains and protein foods that work for you. Or, use the fast as a springboard into a particular kind of diet that you want to follow for health improvement, weight loss or weight management.
- Avoid junk food and overeating. Hopefully, after the fast you will have less desire for unhealthy foods.

4. Resume your Mangosteen Maintenance Dose.

MORE ABOUT THE MANGOSTEEN FAST METHOD #1:

During the fast, vary your doses by mixing them with different amounts of water. This will keep the fast more interesting. Also experiment by Sipping your doses (page 19) or taking them All at Once (page 21). This will help you find out what works best to curb your appetite when you feel hungry. For example, you might find that sipping an undiluted dose works best, or that drinking a glassful of a mangosteen-water mixture all at once is more effective.

The suggested six to twelve ounces a day of mangosteen is a relatively large amount, but it gives your body nutritional and detoxification support during the fast.

You may fast for up to ten days if you are feeling well and are enjoying the effects of the fast. On the other hand, fasting for only one or two days at a time may be best to keep yourself and your life in balance. In my experience, fasting is most effective if done for at least three days.

Fasting helps the body clean out toxins and rebalances all body systems. Mangosteen also has special properties that can enhance the immune system and help the body clear itself of yeast, fungus, parasites, bacteria and viruses.

Before you start a fast of any kind, consult a health-care professional who can let you know if fasting is safe for someone in your particular health condition. This is particularly important if you have never fasted before.

If you are not accustomed to fasting, or if this is your first fast, try it for no more than three days. This is a reasonable time guideline to start with.

The Mangosteen Fast Method #1 can be intense. Consider doing it while you are on vacation, so that you can get all the extra rest your body may need. If this fast seems too intense for you, consider the Mangosteen Fast Method #2 (page 89).

During any fast, try the Mangosteen Enema (page 203). This will help your body flush the toxins, parasites and intestinal-wall buildup that the fast is helping your body to release.

If cleansing reactions (page 233) occur during the fast, drink more water (with mangosteen added) to help your body flush toxins. Also, give yourself more rest and try deep breathing exercises (see the Anti-Stress Procedure on page 53).

Section 1: Drinking Applications

27.

The Mangosteen Fast #2

Here is an easier version of the Mangosteen Fast

USE THE MANGOSTEEN FAST METHOD #2 IF YOU:

- Want the benefits of fasting but don't want to stop eating.
- Have health challenges or a body constitution that doesn't permit you to stop eating.
- Want to limit the risk of possibly initiating an uncomfortable cleansing reaction.

HOW TO FAST WITH MANGOSTEEN USING METHOD #2:

During this fast, you will replace all the liquid in your diet (including water, coffee, tea, juice, soda pop, milk products, beer and alcoholic beverages) with a mixture of mangosteen and water.

1. Decide how much mangosteen you want to take each day during the fast. Your decision may be based on your state of health and how much mangosteen you think your body needs, as well as economics. Certainly try to take at least two or three more ounces of mangosteen than you usually drink each day, and as many as about four to six.

2. Then, for convenience, pre-measure your mangosteen-water mixture as follows:

   a. Find a pitcher, bottle or jar that can contain two quarts (eight cups) of liquid. (Or, find two one-quart containers.) Fill the containers with water. Use spring water, distilled water or purified water.

   b. Gently shake a sealed bottle of mangosteen upside down until the pulp and rind are well mixed throughout the juice.

   c. Measure the daily dosage of mangosteen that you chose in Step 1. Add this to your container of water.

3. Drink the entire amount of the mangosteen-water mixture in one day. Spread the doses throughout the day and take some whenever you are thirsty. You need not drink this on an empty stomach. If you need more to drink, pour a glass of water and add at least a teaspoonful of mangosteen.

MORE ABOUT THE MANGOSTEEN FAST #2:

This fast is easier to do if you prepare your entire daily dose of mangosteen-water ahead of time. Store the container you have used in the refrigerator to keep the mangosteen-water fresh. Pour a glassful whenever you want. Sip or drink all at once.

Try this fast for three days at a time. Fasting any longer is more likely to initiate a cleansing reaction.

You may continue to eat during this fast. For best results, focus your diet on fresh vegetables and fruits, whole grains, and protein foods that work for you. Avoid refined sugar, white flour, saturated fat, hydrogenated oil, food stimulants such as chocolate, as well as food additives and preservatives and processed foods.

People often lose weight while fasting. Since foods are not limited with this fast weight loss may or may not occur. Simply eliminating processed foods and "empty" calories and eating healthy foods, however, often results in weight loss. If you would like to lose weight, also try sipping a glassful of the mangosteen-water mixture when you feel hungry. This may curb your appetite.

Section 1: Drinking Applications

When you are doing the Mangosteen Fast #2, your usual daily doses of mangosteen are replaced by the mangosteen-water doses suggested in this chapter.

The exact amount of mangosteen in each pitcher of water can vary from day to day if you would like to experiment, or change the amount based on how you feel or based on your supply of mangosteen. Also, add some herbal tea or a few drops of lemon juice for flavor. (See Mangosteen Tea and Iced Mangosteen Tea on page 75)

Section 1: Drinking Applications

28.

The Mangosteen Detoxification Program

This method utilizes the body's rhythms for a powerful effect.

USE THE MANGOSTEEN DETOXIFICATION PROGRAM IF YOU:

- Would like the benefits of fasting without having to limit your diet.
- Are relatively healthy and can handle a cleansing reaction, or if you have the support to help you through one.
- Would like to carefully control the detoxification process.

HOW TO DO THE MANGOSTEEN DETOXIFICATION PROGRAM:

To do this program, you will be taking a sip of mangosteen at regular intervals for a chosen number of hours each day for a chosen number of days. For example, you might choose to take a sip every fifteen minutes between noon and 3:00 P.M., every day for four days.

65 Ways to Use Mangosteen

Here is how to design your Mangosteen Detoxification Program:

1. Read about the Three Variables of the Mangosteen Detoxification Program below. Then choose each variable: 1) a time interval between mangosteen sips, 2) the number of hours per day you want to do the program, and 3) for how many days you would like to do the program. During the fast, you can modify these selections based on how you feel. Use the spaces below to write down your initial choices:

What time interval?_____
How many hours per day?_____
How may days?_____

2. When you are ready to begin the fast, pour an ounce of mangosteen, take a sip and mark what time it is.

3. Set a timer to alert you when to take your next dose based on the time interval you chose in Step 1.

4. When the timer rings, take your next sip.

5. Repeat Steps 3 and 4 for the amount of time you chose in Step 1.

THE THREE VARIABLES OF THE MANGOSTEEN DETOXIFICATION PROGRAM:

The Time Interval:
This can be as frequent as a few minutes or as long as one hour. The more frequent the intervals, the more intense the detoxification will be and the more attention you will have to give to the procedure.

How Many Hours per Day you want to do the Program:
This can be as short as about thirty minutes or as long as about twelve hours. However, it must be long enough that you are able to take at least four doses. Select a duration that you can commit to for the number of days that you want to do this

program. You may opt to cut back the duration if you begin to feel that the detoxification is becoming too intense.

How Many Days:

The number of days you would like to continue this program can be one day or up to about fourteen. You may choose to modify this number depending on how you feel. If cleansing symptoms arise, stop. If you are feeling better, consider continuing for an additional few days.

MORE ABOUT THE MANGOSTEEN DETOXIFICATION PROGRAM:

Do not underestimate the power of this program. It can bring on an intense cleansing reaction as your body adjusts to a higher level of health. In addition, you may feel a sense of increasing intensity with every sip you take, especially when your body realizes the rhythm you have initiated. It doesn't take long before your body begins to detoxify. For example, your bowels may become more active, your appetite may decrease, and you may become either more restful or more energized depending on what's going on in your body at the time. (See a list of possible cleansing reactions on pages 233 and 234.)

This detoxification program is powerful because taking a healthful substance like mangosteen at pre-defined intervals establishes a rhythm that can reset the body's rhythms. A healthy body is accustomed to regularity of all its functions and cycles. As our health declines, our rhythms and cycles start to break down. They weaken and become less reliable. The Mangosteen Detoxification Program forces the body into rhythm by regularly presenting it with mangosteen. The body responds very quickly to this rhythm. It uses the rhythm like a template, which encourages the body's natural rhythms to tighten up and become more regular. Interestingly, it does not seem to matter what kind of rhythm one establishes for this program. People will design the program in a way that not only suits their schedule, but I suspect that whatever they design will also be the perfect template for their body's systems.

The first thing that usually happens when the body's rhythms are tightened is that the cells initiate a cleansing. Yet you can control how quickly this cleansing occurs. To alleviate cleansing reactions, cut back the amount of time each day that you do the program. To intensify the detox, increase the amount of time per day that you do the program. Once you start, however, don't adjust the time interval between doses because this determines the rhythm which is key to this program's effectiveness.

During this program, use your regular daily doses of mangosteen. In the morning, measure your entire daily dose—the total amount you want to take that day—and pour it into a drinking glass. Then sip from the glass. If you have some mangosteen left over, drink it up when it's time to take your last sip of the day.

Section 1: Drinking Applications

29.

Adding Mangosteen to Recipes

Mangosteen tastes good all by itself. But sometimes children and other family members may object to taking supplements no matter the taste. An option is to hide mangosteen in food. You may also want to add mangosteen to food if the daily dosage your body requires is more than you can comfortably drink. (For example, if you are following the Procedure for Health Improvement #2 on page 41.)

Remember to shake the bottle of mangosteen upside down before pouring a dose, in order to mix the rind particles thoroughly with the rest of the juice.

Here are some recipe ideas:

Sauces and Spreads:
- Add one ounce of mangosteen to a bottle of blueberry sauce and shake to mix the ingredients together. Pour this on cheesecake, pancakes or waffles. If the blueberry sauce contains bits of blueberry skin, the mangosteen rind particles should be well disguised.

- Add one-half to one teaspoonful of mangosteen juice per serving of any prepared or home-cooked sauce after it has been cooked or heated. If the sauce contains herbs then the mangosteen rind particles should go unnoticed. Otherwise, strain the rind before adding the mangosteen to the sauce.

- Add an ounce of mangosteen to the ketchup bottle and shake well. Straining the mangosteen is essential in this case. Otherwise the kids are sure to object.

- Add about one tablespoonful of mangosteen to the jelly jar and mix. If the jelly has seeds, such as raspberry, strawberry or blackberry, you might be able to get away without straining the mangosteen. If you use grape jelly, definitely strain the particles.

- Here's how to make Mangosteen-rich Peanut butter and Jelly Sandwiches:

This sandwich provides a larger portion of mangosteen than using jelly mixed with mangosteen juice. Spread one slice of bread with peanut butter as usual. Spread the other slice of bread with a thin layer (about one-eighth to one-quarter teaspoonful), of Mangosteen Paste (see page 173). Cover the paste with your child's favorite jelly. The Mangosteen Paste will be hardly detectable, especially if you use chunky peanut-butter or whole-grain bread. If your kids insist on smooth peanut butter and white bread, use Smooth Mangosteen Paste (page 177).

Soups:
Add one or two teaspoonfuls of mangosteen per serving of canned or homemade soup after cooking or heating. You can also add it to cold gazpacho or fruit soups. If the soup contains herbs or vegetables, or has a thick consistency, you may not need to strain the mangosteen. Mangosteen rind particles can be an artistic touch at the bottom of a bowl of clear soup or broth.

Salads and Dressings:
- Add an ounce of mangosteen to any commercial salad dressing bottle. Shake well before serving.
- Add a teaspoonful of mangosteen per serving of fresh fruit salad or canned fruit cocktail. In this case, it is best to strain the mangosteen and use only the juice.

- Try one-half teaspoonful of strained mangosteen per cup of potato salad. Mix it with the mayonnaise before stirring the mayonnaise into the potatoes.

- One-half to one teaspoonful of mangosteen (strain if necessary) can also be added per serving of tuna salad. Gently mix the mangosteen with the tuna before adding the other ingredients.

Grains and pasta:
- After cooking white rice, add one-half to one ounce of mangosteen. Use a fork to fluff the rice and mix in the juice. The rind particles can look attractive in the rice, especially if you also garnish it with chopped scallions. The rind will practically disappear if you garnish with black sesame seeds.

- Also add mangosteen juice to cooked whole grains. Add sesame seeds, coconut, nuts and/or raisins to complement the fruity flavor.

- Sprinkle a few teaspoonfuls of mangosteen over a cup of stuffing, after it has been cooked and removed from the turkey.

- Pasta that is dressed with tomato-based sauce can be a fool-proof way to hide mangosteen. The fruity mangosteen sweetens the tomato sauce and gives it added flavor and richness. If your sauce contains plenty of herbs, the rind particles will be well hidden and you won't need to strain the mangosteen. You should be able to add one teaspoonful to one tablespoonful of mangosteen per serving (larger servings and thicker sauces can handle the larger amount) without anyone detecting mangosteen's presence.

Vegetables:
- Cook sweet potatoes or yams. Mash them with butter, honey, cinnamon and a teaspoonful of strained mangosteen per serving.

- Add mangosteen to stir-fried vegetables after they have been cooked. Use a teaspoonful per serving.

- Add one or two teaspoonfuls of mangosteen per cup of cold green bean salad.

65 Ways to Use Mangosteen

- Saute leafy greens such as chard, collards or kale. Add mushrooms and or onions for flavor. When done cooking, add one-half to one teaspoonful of mangosteen per serving.

- Also try mixing one-half to one teaspoonful of mangosteen per serving of baked beans, refried beans or chili after these dishes have been cooked. The mangosteen may or may not need to be strained, depending on your preference and whether or not the other ingredients in your recipe will hide the rind particles.

Meat, Fish and Poultry:
Pour one-half teaspoonful of mangosteen over each serving of meat, fish or poultry after it has been cooked.

Desserts:
- Mix one teaspoonful of strained mangosteen per serving of chocolate sauce for a delicious ice cream topping.

- Make homemade ice cream flavored with mangosteen (strained or unstrained) and other fruits and berries.

- Add a teaspoonful of mangosteen to unsweetened yogurt. Mix in chunks of fruit or berries and a bit of honey. Top with nuts or wheat germ.

- Add up to one tablespoonful of mangosteen per cup of spiced apple cider. You won't need to strain the mangosteen, as the spices used in mulled cider tend to sink to the bottom of the cup and will blend with the rind particles.

- Sprinkle an ounce of mangosteen over fruit pies and cobblers after cooking.

- Add strained mangosteen to other fruit juices, and serve as fruit juice or freeze into fruit popsicles.

HOW TO USE LEFTOVER MANGOSTEEN RIND PARTICLES:

Despite mangosteen's good taste, some people have trouble swallowing the mangosteen rind particles, or complain that the particles get stuck in their teeth. In particular, children rarely tolerate drinking the rind particles. Children can also be picky eaters and object to finding the particles in their food. For this reason, many of the recipe ideas in this chapter suggest straining the mangosteen rind and using the liquid part of mangosteen juice only.

If you are using only about one-half to one teaspoonful of mangosteen, there won't be that many rind particles to strain. This will be especially true if you are using a newly-opened mangosteen bottle. No matter how diligent we are at shaking the bottle to distribute the pulp and rind particles before we pour a dose, there always seems to be more particles per dose when the bottle is half empty or less.

Still, to successfully hide mangosteen in certain foods, you will need to strain the particles. Use a strainer with very fine mesh. Another option, which is even more effective, is to start by filling a one-ounce medicine cup with mangosteen. Wait a few minutes for the rind particles to sink to the bottom of the medicine cup. Then carefully pour the juice you need off the top. Drink the remaining pulp and rind particles as part of your daily dose of mangosteen. Or, save it for another recipe. Strained mangosteen rind particles should be stored in the refrigerator unless they are completely dry.

Here are some ideas for using mangosteen rind particles:

- Use them as a garnish. Sprinkle them on any light-colored food which will provide a good contrast for the dark purple particles. (For example, yogurt, cheesecake, ice cream, casseroles, potato salad, cream soups, tofu and chicken.)
- Hide them in any crunchy food such as granola and salads, or with ground nuts that you can then use in a variety of ways.
- Supercharge your daily dose of mangosteen that you usually drink by adding the rind particles to it.
- Add them to dried herbal preparations and combinations.

Or,

- Add them to your pet's food. (See Giving Mangosteen to Pets on page 107.)
- Mix the rind particles with body lotion for exfoliating purposes. (See page 145.)
- Use them to make a Mangosteen Decoction (page 79) which is a traditional remedy for diarrhea and cystitis.
- Use them to make the Mangosteen Tooth and Gum Pack (page 223).
- Use them for the Mangosteen Toe Treatment (page 197).

MORE ABOUT ADDING MANGOSTEEN TO RECIPES:

The amounts of mangosteen suggested for the recipes in this chapter are suggestions only. Adjust the amount to suit your taste and preference. In general, recipes can easily incorporate one-half to one teaspoonful of mangosteen per serving. Mangosteen lends a subtle sweet and tangy flavor, which blends well with a wide variety of food.

How much mangosteen you can add to a recipe depends on how well the juice combines with the other ingredients and how important it is to hide the presence of mangosteen (especially for children). If you love the taste of mangosteen, as many people do, add mangosteen freely to your recipes, rind particles and all.

It is best not to take your entire daily dose of mangosteen in foods, as you will get the most from mangosteen's healing compounds if you drink it on an empty stomach.

Add mangosteen to foods after they have been cooked. This will preserve the heat sensitive healing compounds in mangosteen.

Section 1: Drinking Applications

30.

Giving Mangosteen to Children

Children can use any of the mangosteen drinking procedures in this book with dose modifications, as well as any of the mangosteen topical applications listed in Section 2.

BABIES AND YOUNG CHILDREN:

Healthy babies and toddlers may not need a daily Maintenance Dose of mangosteen. However, if you feel your children could benefit from a Maintenance Dose, try one-half to one teaspoonful a day. This can easily be added to your child's favorite fruit juice and your youngster may hardly know it's there. Interrupt Mangosteen Therapy (page 67) often, perhaps every two months for one or two weeks at a time. Or just give them doses on weekdays.

During times of illness and stress, you may indeed want to supplement your children's diet with mangosteen. Choose drinking procedures appropriate for your child's condition, then modify the dosages. In general, give babies and toddlers one-sixth to one-quarter of each dose amount suggested for adults. (When figuring dosages, it may help to know that one ounce contains six teaspoonfuls.) If they crave mangosteen, let them drink as much as about one-half cup—but not everyday.

When you feel your baby is getting sick or has been exposed to a contagious illness, try the suggested dose for Sick-Day Prevention (page 59) which is one tablespoonful two or three times a day. For a tonic during times of stress (page 83) give one or two extra teaspoonfuls in addition to any Maintenance Dose you may be already giving them.

If an infant is breastfeeding, give the mother extra mangosteen. Like many supplements, mangosteen's healing compounds should pass through the breastmilk.

Strain the rind particles from doses of mangosteen that you give babies who are drinking fruit juices, but who are not yet eating solid foods. A child should not be given unstrained mangosteen until their digestive systems are able to handle the pulp and rind.

Use topical applications such as the Mangosteen Mini-Poultice (page 169) freely. For rashes, try the Mangosteen Hand and Body Lotion (page 161) first, which should be more gentle on a baby's skin than the Rash Plaster (page 183).

OLDER CHILDREN:

Older children deal with a lot of stress these days, including the pressures of school, changing domestic environments and the distractions of a technological world. Pollution, particularly from school bus exhaust, poses a widespread problem, as well as the additives found in our food and water. For these reasons and more, a daily Maintenance Dose is recommended for children as a preventive measure. Children may need only two or three teaspoonfuls of mangosteen a day.

Children can follow any of the drinking procedures in this book, with dose modifications. For example, those with chronic health challenges such as asthma, chronic ear infections or behavioral challenges can follow the Procedures for Chronic Conditions (page 37). Take about one-quarter to one-half the dose suggested for adults. (Parents, adjust doses based on your child's body weight relative to that of the average adult.)

Children who get the flu or become ill or injured could benefit from the Sick-Day Prevention Dose (page 59), which is about one ounce of mangosteen two or three times a day. For relatively mild acute conditions, sometimes just one two-ounce dose may be all they need to alleviate early symptoms.

You may also want to give your child extra mangosteen to support their immune system before a vacation, before school begins, or before a recital or other presentation, etc. The chapter on the Mangosteen Tonic (page 83) suggests giving children one extra tablespoonful in the days prior to a stressful event, as well as immediately before that stressful event occurs.

Healthy children should Interrupt Mangosteen Therapy (page 67) often, perhaps every two months for one or two weeks at a time. Or just give your child doses on weekdays. Children who take mangosteen for a chronic condition, like asthma, might Interrupt Mangosteen Therapy for only a few days every month.

SECRETS FOR SUCCESSFULLY GIVING MANGOSTEEN TO CHILDREN:

- First impressions are important. Make sure your child's first experience taking mangosteen is a positive one. A fool proof way to make the dose palatable (if not also enjoyable) is by mixing it with another juice beverage. Use a brand of juice they haven't tried before, so they won't be familiar with the taste.
- Don't expect your children to balk—they may really like mangosteen!
- Act naturally—don't make a fuss over giving them their doses.
- Hide mangosteen in foods. (See Adding Mangosteen to Recipes on page 97.)
- If necessary, don't let them know you've put mangosteen in their juice or food.

TEENAGERS:

When children enter the pre-teen and teen years, they could benefit from a daily dose of mangosteen. It may ease the effects of the many hormonal and physical transitions their bodies are making.

Offer them mangosteen everyday when you drink your doses to accustom them to a routine and to a lifestyle that includes mangosteen. If they refuse to drink any, at least let them see that you take mangosteen daily and apply it topically when needed.

If teens are not forced to use mangosteen, they will be more willing to take it. Still, they may watch what mangosteen does for their parents first before they try it themselves. Let them know it is available for them. Instead of following a daily maintenance regimen, teens may prefer to take mangosteen "as needed." Tell them that mangosteen can be used both orally and topically to help conditions that are of particular concern to teens. For example, mangosteen can help clear the skin, stabilize mood swings, enhance athletic performance, improve stamina, speed recovery time for athletic injuries, help overcome common cold and flu symptoms, and aid mental clarity and focus.

For both maintenance and for illnesses, teens may follow the same procedures and take the same dosages as adults. Teens who weigh less than one hundred pounds could start with half the suggested amounts. For the occasional tonic before stressful events teens could take one extra ounce a day on the days prior to the event. (See the Mangosteen Tonic on page 83.) For Sick-Day Prevention, a suggested dose is two ounces, two or three times a day.

> Parents should use their common sense, intuition and best judgment when giving mangosteen to their children, and should consult a health-care professional whenever necessary.

Section 1: Drinking Applications

31.
Giving Mangosteen to Pets

The following tips for giving mangosteen to pets are not meant to replace your veterinarian's advice, but to be used in addition to the therapies your vet suggests.

Our pets can benefit from the healing compounds in mangosteen just as much as human beings can. Generally, the effects of mangosteen on their bodies will be the same as the effects on ours. Because their body size is usually much smaller, dosage amounts need to be adjusted accordingly.

TIPS FOR GIVING MANGOSTEEN TO CATS:

Young healthy cats probably don't need a Maintenance Dose, but as your cat gets older definitely consider giving her one. Animals are often unable to communicate their aches and pains, or else we are unable to read what they're trying to tell us. A Mangosteen Maintenance Dose can alleviate mild symptoms, boost your cat's immune system and help prevent disease.

A Maintenance Dose for cats can be about one-quarter to one-half teaspoonful of mangosteen per day. Add this amount to your cat's food. If necessary, start with one-eighth teaspoonful and gradually increase the dose as your cat becomes accustomed to it. Mangosteen does not have a strong aroma and may pass unnoticed. Likely, if your cat is accustomed to dry food, and you give her wet food with a dose of mangosteen mixed in it, she will love it regardless.

When measuring such small doses for your cat, start by pouring a one-ounce dose. (Make sure to first shake the mangosteen bottle upside down for awhile to thoroughly mix the rind particles with the juice.) Then, using a one-quarter teaspoon, briefly mix the one-ounce dose to disperse the rind, and then scoop out a dose for your cat. This way your cat's dose will have a balanced mixture of mangosteen pulp and rind. Drink the remainder of the dose yourself, including it as part of your own total daily dosage of mangosteen.

If your cat becomes ill, but is still eating, increase the daily dosage of mangosteen that you put in her food. If she is unable to eat, refuses the higher dosage in her food, or has a condition that warrants taking mangosteen on an empty stomach, you will have to inject the dose into the back of her mouth. To do this you will need an eyedropper or small plastic syringe tube. Eyedroppers come in different sizes, so to know exactly how much mangosteen you are giving your cat, pre-measure the total daily amount you want to give her. Then draw from this amount throughout the day. Your cat may prefer room temperature mangosteen so keep the dose on the countertop. A day outside the refrigerator won't spoil it.

Giving mangosteen to cats via eyedropper or syringe can be challenging and will take practice. It helps to tip your cat's head up and hold it there before quickly injecting the mangosteen into the back of her mouth. You may have to gently pry open her teeth. Help her swallow the mangosteen by stroking her throat with the side of your finger. Stroke her throat in a downward motion, in order to enhance her swallowing reflex.

The following dose guidelines are suggestions only. Use your intuition and common sense to decide how much mangosteen to give your cat. Be sure to visit your vet if your cat's condition is serious.

DOSE GUIDELINES FOR CATS:

- For injuries, apply mangosteen directly to the wound. Also give your cat as much as one tablespoonful of mangosteen two or three times a day. This serves as a Trauma Dose (page 57).
- For chronic conditions, try one-half to one teaspoonful of mangosteen two or three times a day.
- For serious conditions, try as much as one or two teaspoonfuls of mangosteen, four to eight times a day.

- A single one tablespoon dose can sometimes be all that is needed to clear relatively minor health conditions.
- Continue mangosteen therapy until the condition improves, then reduce the dosage to a maintenance level.

MANGOSTEEN TREATS FOR CATS AND DOGS:

Here is a simple recipe for making treats filled with your pet's daily dose of mangosteen. They are preferred if you have more than one pet eating at the food bowl, and will allow you to be certain exactly how much mangosteen your pet receives.

1. In a small bowl, use a fork to mash one tablespoonful of tuna fish or fish leftovers. These are strong-smelling foods which should completely mask the mangosteen, however you could also try wet cat or dog food or raw ground meat.

2. Mix in one teaspoonful of mangosteen and two teaspoonfuls of flour.

3. The mixture will be soft, but should hold together just enough to form into one or more balls. Double or triple the amount of mangosteen and flour you use if your pet needs more mangosteen. To supply a cat's smaller daily Maintenance Dose, give her only a portion of the recipe as needed to satisfy her daily dosage.

TIPS FOR GIVING MANGOSTEEN TO DOGS:

You could give your dog a Maintenance Dose in his food, but when using mangosteen to alleviate health conditions, mangosteen is best taken on an empty stomach either by itself or with water. Start by offering him a dose in a bowl mixed with an amount of water that he will drink at one time. If your dog likes mangosteen, you could also try giving him doses in a bowl without water. If these ideas don't work you will have to put his dose of mangosteen directly into his mouth using a plastic syringe tube:

1. Fill a plastic syringe tube (available at pet stores) with a dose of mangosteen.

2. Have your dog sit.

3. Position yourself beside your dog's right shoulder (assuming you are right-handed). Stand or kneel, depending on your dog's size. Hold the syringe in your right hand. Show him the syringe and let him sniff it. Give him lots of pats and praise.

4. Wrap your left arm around your dog's shoulder and slide your left hand under his chin. Gently lift his chin so that he is looking up. He may respond by kissing you.

5. Insert the end of the syringe inside the back corner of his cheek. Use either the right or left side of his face, whichever side works best for you. The end of the syringe should be pointing down, between the inside of his cheek and his teeth. Your left hand should be underneath his lower jaw, gently keeping his chin pointed toward the ceiling. You don't need to open his mouth as you will be inserting the mangosteen inside his cheek and not between his teeth.

6. Squeeze the mangosteen into his mouth between his cheek and his teeth as fast as he will drink it. He will use his tongue to lap it up. The trick is to keep his nose pointing up, the syringe pointing down, and to work quickly. Reassure him by talking to him constantly and looking kindly in his eyes. Have patience and always praise. Sooner or later, you will be able to give him mangosteen without spilling a drop—or maybe only one or two!

DOSE GUIDELINES FOR DOGS:

Evaluate your dog's condition as you might evaluate your own and select from the drinking applications in this book. You may need to modify the procedures to suit him and some just won't work for pets. (Can you imagine your dog doing the Mangosteen Gargle!)

Section 1: Drinking Application

Dogs that weigh more than one hundred pounds can receive the same dosage amounts as humans. Give medium-size dogs the same amount you would give children, and small dogs the same amount you would give babies and young children (page 103).

Dosages for animals are usually measured in CCs. Your plastic syringe tube may therefore list only CCs. Here are the equivalents:

5CCs = one teaspoonful = 5ml.
15CCs = one tablespoonful = 1/2 ounce = 15ml.
30CCs = one ounce = 30ml.
60CCs = two ounces = 60ml.

65 Ways to Use Mangosteen

Section 1: Drinking Application

32.

Keeping Mangosteen a Family Friend

Here are some ways to keep mangosteen useful after the initial excitement of adding it to your diet wears off.

THE IDEAS IN THIS CHAPTER CAN BE HELPFUL FOR:

- All members of the family.
- General health maintenance.
- The long-time mangosteen enthusiast.
- And when the mangosteen bottle starts to drift to the back of the refrigerator.

HOW TO KEEP MANGOSTEEN A FAMILY FRIEND:

Here are some ideas for incorporating mangosteen into your lifestyle:
- Make a ritual of giving everyone in the family their daily dose of mangosteen at the same time and place.
- When illness occurs, remember mangosteen. At the first sign of colds or flu, make it a habit to take a Sick-Day Prevention Dose (page 59).

- Let your children observe how you reach for mangosteen whenever you need health support.
- Let the phrase, "Time for some mangosteen" become common language in your household.
- Become familiar with the applications described in this book. Experiment with them and find out which work best for you. When a situation arises that calls for one of these procedures, you will be more comfortable using it if you have experimented with it beforehand.
- Let your children help you make and apply various topical applications. Children particularly enjoy making Mini-poultices (page 169).
- Involve your children in the making of Mangosteen Paste. Let them watch how the juice changes as the water evaporates. Let them taste some of the paste. How sweet it is!
- Use Mangosteen Lotion daily.
- Each time your shipment of mangosteen arrives, make a habit of preparing batches of various mangosteen products that you and your family can easily reach for in the coming weeks. For example, Mangosteen Hand and Body Lotion (page 161), Mangosteen Abdominal Conditioner (page 123), Mangosteen Analgesic Ointment (page 131), Mangosteen Deodorant (page 141) and Mangosteen Astringent and Aftershave (page 127)
- Experiment with adding mangosteen to foods (see Adding Mangosteen to Recipes on page 97).
- Always add some mangosteen to your family's pitcher of iced tea.
- Make it a habit to turn to mangosteen whenever a health condition arises. Always "remember mangosteen."
- Keep at least two extra bottles of mangosteen available for emergencies and sick days, when everyone in the family may need extra doses. (See The Mangosteen Tonic on page 83, and The Mangosteen Sick-Day Prevention Dose on page 59.)
- Continue to try new ways to use Mangosteen. (See The Maintenance Dose #3 on page 29.) Feel free to modify and adapt the procedures in this book to suit your individual needs and preferences.
- Keep this book handy for reference.

MORE ABOUT KEEPING MANGOSTEEN A FAMILY FRIEND:

Mangosteen is here to help you and your family. It is a gift of nature. All you have to do is be willing to try it, use it and keep looking for new ways that it can help you. It is important to be creative and flexible with mangosteen and be ever willing to experiment and try new ways to work with it. The ideas in this book give you an excellent start. Finally, the most effective way to maintain (if not also increase) your excitement and enthusiasm about mangosteen is to share it with others. (See Sharing a First Dose with Others on page 117).

Section 1: Drinking Applications

33.

Sharing a First Dose with Others

Find out how satisfying it can be to share a good thing with your family and friends.

SHARE A FIRST DOSE WITH OTHERS:

- Who have a health challenge that you think mangosteen might aid.
- Who are interested in what you are doing to improve your own health.
- When you have a health benefit from mangosteen that you can offer as a personal testimonial.
- When you would like to offer your friends a supportive environment when taking their first dose.

HOW TO SHARE A FIRST DOSE WITH OTHERS:

Here are some ideas for inviting your family and friends to try a dose of mangosteen.

- Invite a few friends over to try a first dose together. Taking a first dose with a group provides a supportive environment. When people share a common experience like this, it can heighten their sensitivity to the immediate effects they feel and magnify the excitement for this healthful product. Follow the steps in the chapter Evaluating the Immediate Effects of Mangosteen, on page 7.

- If you notice that a friend or family member has a skin condition, suggest they try mangosteen topically. See The Easy Mangosteen Skin Conditioner on page 195. Rashes treated with mangosteen often show improvement within minutes.
- Let houseguests see how you incorporate mangosteen into your family life. See Keeping Mangosteen a Family Friend on page 113.
- Know your Health Index number (page 227) and how it has improved since you began taking mangosteen. This can be an excellent conversation starter.
- Another easy way to introduce people to mangosteen is to use my booklet, "Getting Started with Mangosteen."* You don't have to do much explaining, just lend people the booklet and let it talk for you. After they've read it, ask them if they have any questions and if they have calculated their Health Index number. Invite them to try some mangosteen to see for themselves how well mangosteen can improve their health and Health Index.
- Share your Mangosteen Story as often as you can. Develop a ten-second, thirty-second and five-minute version to meet a variety of circumstances in which you may find yourself. Keep in mind that when you share mangosteen with others, you are helping them write the first chapter of their own Mangosteen Story.

YOUR MANGOSTEEN STORY:

Everyone who has had any success with mangosteen has a story to tell. Do not underestimate the importance of your story. It is something that you started to write the moment you heard about mangosteen. You add a new chapter with each improvement in your health. Your mangosteen story is your legacy. It should inspire others when they hear it, and re-inspire you each time you tell it!

What to Include in Your Mangosteen Story:
- How you found out about mangosteen.
- How you took your first dose, what improvements you noticed immediately and what you began to notice over time.
- How mangosteen has helped you and your family.
- The information on your Health Index Summary Sheet (page 232), and how it has given you objective evidence that mangosteen has indeed been improving your health.

* Available from Direct Source. Call: 1-800-461-7090.

MORE ABOUT SHARING MANGOSTEEN WITH OTHERS:

There are endless ways to introduce others to a healthier lifestyle and to a healthful supplement like mangosteen. This chapter outlines only a few. I include them in this book to emphasize how important it is to be a living example of a healthy lifestyle. Sharing mangosteen with others not only gives them an opportunity to explore greater health, it also gives you the incentive to stay on course, keep up the good work and continue to pursue and demonstrate health and happiness.

SECTION 2
Topical Applications of Mangosteen

The following chapters suggest topical applications of mangosteen that can improve the health of the skin, as well as help the body heal, repair and strengthen organs and other tissue inside the body. For skin conditions, mangosteen's healing compounds work directly on the treated area. To address conditions inside the body, mangosteen's healing compounds must penetrate the skin. Then the body seems to be able to transport these compounds to the areas that need them.

Drinking mangosteen enhances the effects of topical applications and vice versa. Therefore, it is always a good idea to combine the two. For example, after you apply a Mangosteen Poultice, drink a dose of mangosteen. Likewise, if the condition for which you are drinking mangosteen has an identifiable location, be sure to apply topical applications there regularly. Applying mangosteen topically also draws to the treatment area the healing compounds of mangosteen taken orally. This gives you some control as to where you want mangosteen to work. Simply apply topical applications to the area that you want the healing compounds of your oral doses to focus on.

The chapters in Section 2 include techniques for using mangosteen for a variety of conditions that are listed at the beginning of each chapter. These conditions and the applications that are designed to treat them, will give you an idea of mangosteen's potential and tremendous scope as a topical application.

As you read through the chapters, you may notice that a few applications can be applied for the same ailments. This helps to ensure that there will be some kind of mangosteen topical treatment for almost everyone. For example, for dermatitis and rashes you can use the Mangosteen Poultice (page 179), the Mangosteen Rash Plaster (page

183), the Easy Mangosteen Skin Conditioner (page 195), the Mangosteen Astringent (page 127) or the Mangosteen Sunburn Treatment (page 191). For small rashes, Mangosteen Paste (page 173) or the Mangosteen Mini-Poultice (page 169) can also be helpful. Therefore, to find topical applications for your particular health concern, begin by checking the index. Then try the various applications suggested to see which work best for you.

The topical applications in the following chapters are listed alphabetically. For an overview, please see the Table of Contents at the beginning of this book.

Section 2: Topical Applications

34.

Mangosteen Abdominal Conditioner

Try this procedure daily—it is as important to your health as brushing your teeth.

USE THIS DAILY TREATMENT TO:

- Alleviate and prevent constipation and intestinal blockages.
- Alleviate intestinal inflammation.
- Alleviate fever.
- Improve the flow of matter through the intestines.
- Improve the general health of the abdominal organs.
- Increase circulation to the abdominal organs.
- Increase the amount of life-giving energy moving through your abdomen, to benefit the organs there.

HOW TO MAKE THE MANGOSTEEN-LOTION MIXTURE FOR THIS TREATMENT:

1. Shake a sealed bottle of mangosteen upside down until the rind particles are completely mixed with the watery part of the juice.

2. Pour an ounce of mangosteen into a medicine cup. Wait for the mangosteen particles to settle to the bottom of the medicine cup. This should take about a minute. Don't wait any longer, as the pulp will also settle to the bottom of the cup, and we want to include the pulp in this treatment.

3. Then carefully measure one teaspoonful of rind-free mangosteen from the top of the medicine cup. Put this teaspoonful of mangosteen into a teacup or a second medicine cup.

4. Use the same measuring spoon to measure one teaspoonful of your favorite body lotion.

5. Use a cotton swab to wipe the body lotion from the teaspoon into the teacup or medicine cup that contains the mangosteen. Then use the same cotton swab to mix the lotion and mangosteen juice together. Mix well.

This recipe will make enough for several treatments—exactly how many treatments depends on the size of your abdomen and how much mangosteen-lotion mixture you use. Keep the mixture beside your bed for convenience. The mixture will stay fresh at room temperature for a day or two if you keep the mixture in an airtight container in a cool, dark place. It will keep fresh longer if the lotion you use contains preservatives.

HOW TO APPLY THE
MANGOSTEEN ABDOMINAL CONDITIONER:

1. Bring the mangosteen-lotion mixture, as well as the cotton swab you used to make it, to your bedroom.

2. Lie down on your back and remove the clothing off your abdomen, from your ribcage down to your pubic bone.

3. Use the cotton swab to scoop up a portion of the mixture you have made, and place it on your abdomen.

4. Using the palms and fingers of both hands, massage the mixture over your entire abdomen from just under your ribs

down to your hips and pubic bone. Apply more mangosteen-lotion mixture if necessary. When you massage:

- Use mostly large sweeping clockwise circles. (Clockwise looking down at your body.) This is the pathway that material travels through your large intestine. Massaging in this way will encourage the movement of this material forward through it.
- Also try working your abdomen in a kneading motion.
- Another idea is to press your fingertips deeply into your belly and make small circles with your fingertips. Do this at several different points on your abdomen and particularly where you have blockages or gas pockets. Be gentle over points of pain.
- Here is one of my favorite abdominal massage movements: Hold your hands on your hips with your fingers pointing toward each other. Your fingers should be in front of your hips and your thumbs in back. Press your fingertips into your abdomen. Massage by bending and straightening your fingers. Then, with your thumbs still holding your hips, keep moving your fingers in this way as you point them lower toward your feet, then upward toward your rib cage and then back down again.

MORE ABOUT THE MANGOSTEEN ABDOMINAL CONDITIONER:

Cover your abdomen generously with the mangosteen-lotion mixture. How much of the mixture you use depends on how large your abdomen is. Experiment to find the amount you need, and then adjust how much you make next time. If you do adjust the recipe, simply use equal parts of mangosteen and lotion.

Apply this treatment once a day as part of your daily health maintenance regimen. It is most effect when done lying down when your abdominal muscles are relaxed. Then it is easier to access your internal organs.

When you first apply the mangosteen-lotion mixture, it will feel slippery. After a minute or two (depending on how much mangosteen-lotion you have used) your skin will begin to feel sticky. End the massage and allow the mixture to soak in and dry. The sticky feeling will then go away, leaving your skin soft and smooth.

If some rind particles accidentally get included in the mangosteen-lotion mixture, they will show up on your abdomen and feel scratchy as you apply the massage. Brush them off or remove them with a tissue.

While applying this treatment you may find pockets of gas, intestinal blockages and painful areas that you didn't know you had. Most people will have a few spots that are tender. Work gently on these areas to release the pockets and open the blockages. Use common sense and work gently on painful areas or even stop the massage if it makes a painful area feel worse. Spread another layer of mangosteen-lotion over this area and let it air dry.

If you have a particular problem area or organ, such as liver disease, stomach or gallbladder distress or colitis or constipation, or, if you're a woman and have problems with your reproductive organs, spread extra mangosteen-lotion mixture over the area. Gently massage it into your skin and then let it air dry.

As the body lotion soaks into the skin, which it is designed to do, mangosteen's healing compounds will soak in along with it. These compounds will eventually migrate to the areas that need them.

After a few treatments, you may notice improvements in your bowel regularity. You'll find fewer gas pockets, and any tender spots you might have should abate or just go away. Part of this relief is due to the massage itself. But a significant source of improvement does indeed come from the mangosteen healing compounds. Mangosteen's anti-inflammatory properties are soothing to many abdominal conditions that are either caused by inflammation or that have inflammation as a primary symptom.

You might also feel more overall energy after several treatments, since the abdomen is the home of the "tantien" which in Chinese Medicine is the source and powerhouse of energy in the body. When you open blockages in the area of the tantien, energy can move around your body more freely, giving you life, health and strength.

Section 2: Topical Applications

35.

Mangosteen Astringent and Aftershave

An astringent draws together or constricts body tissues and is effective for stopping the flow of blood or other secretions. This makes it perfect for use as an aftershave as well as for first aid.

TRY THE MANGOSTEEN ASTRINGENT AND AFTERSHAVE:

- As you would regular aftershave: on the face, legs or underarms.
- For skin that gets irritated or dry from shaving.
- As a first aid application for abrasions, cuts, scrapes and other minor wounds.

ALSO MAKE INTO A POULTICE FOR:

- Bruises.
- Burns and scalds.
- Dermatitis.
- Inflammation.
- Insect bites.
- Swelling.

HOW TO MAKE MANGOSTEEN ASTRINGENT AND AFTERSHAVE:

This procedure incorporates mangosteen with the popular witch hazel astringent cleanser, which contains approximately 14% alcohol plus witch hazel distillate and witch hazel extract.

1. Obtain an empty four-ounce plastic bottle from the drug store. Such bottles are commonly used to transport shampoo or hand lotion when traveling.

2. Shake a sealed bottle of mangosteen upside down until the rind particles are well mixed with the rest of the juice. Pour one ounce into a one-ounce medicine cup. Wait a few minutes for the rind particles to settle to the bottom of the medicine cup.

3. Measure one teaspoonful of particle-free juice from the top of the medicine cup. Pour it into the plastic bottle.

4. Measure one tablespoonful (three teaspoonfuls) of witch hazel astringent cleanser and add this to the plastic bottle. Shake the bottle to mix the two ingredients together.

MORE ABOUT MANGOSTEEN ASTRINGENT AND AFTERSHAVE:

The amounts suggested in the recipe above should be enough for several aftershave treatments. It is also a small enough quantity that you will probably use it up within a few days, and therefore you can leave it outside the refrigerator. Store it in a cool, dark place, such as inside a medicine cabinet.

If you are applying this formula as a poultice for injuries or dermatitis, try adding two or three teaspoonfuls of mangosteen to the one tablespoonful of witch hazel. However these proportions will make the application feel sticky. Though the stickiness goes away after the mangosteen-witch hazel mixture dries, this larger proportion of mangosteen would not be popular as an aftershave. Use it for first aid purposes only.

Section 2: Topical Applications

Witch hazel is a medicinal herb, whose distillate/extract can be found in most drug stores or health food stores. According to Mrs. M. Grieve, author of *A Modern Herbal, Volume II*, witch hazel has been used by the North American Indians as poultices for painful swellings and tumors. It is also helpful for bruises and inflammatory swellings, insect bites, burns, scalds, varicose veins, dermatitis, and to help stop bleeding.*

Combining the healing properties of witch hazel with the anti-inflammatory, antiseptic and anti-histamine properties of mangosteen, gives us a powerful therapeutic formula helpful for a variety of ailments. Keep some on hand at all times, and store it in the refrigerator unless you plan to use it daily as aftershave.

---

* Grieve, Mrs. M., *A Modern Herbal, Volume II*, (New York, NY: Dover Publications), 1971, page 851.

36.

Mangosteen Analgesic Ointment

A concentrated remedy for acute and chronic pain.

TRY MANGOSTEEN ANALGESIC OINTMENT FOR CONDITIONS WITH LOCALIZED PAIN SUCH AS:

- Arthritis.
- Back pain.
- Carpal tunnel syndrome.
- Endometriosis.
- Fibromyalgia.
- Foot pain.
- Inflammation.
- Injuries (where the skin is unbroken).
- Joint pain.
- Muscle spasms.
- Neuralgia.
- Rough, cracked skin.
- Sprains.

HOW TO MAKE
MANGOSTEEN ANALGESIC OINTMENT:

1. Make a recipe of Smooth Mangosteen Paste as described on page 177, starting with one ounce of mangosteen juice.

2. Measure the amount of Smooth Paste you have made with a measuring spoon.

3. Use a cotton swab to wipe the Smooth Mangosteen Paste off the measuring spoon and into a small airtight container.

4. Use the same measuring spoon to measure an equal amount of your favorite body lotion. (The paste-lotion mixture you are making should have equal parts of Smooth Mangosteen Paste and body lotion.)

5. Use the cotton swab to remove the lotion from the measuring spoon and put it into the container of paste. Then use the cotton swab to mix the paste and lotion together. Mix well. You have now made Mangosteen Analgesic Ointment.

6. Use the cotton swab to dab some of the Mangosteen Analgesic Ointment onto the area you want to treat. Again, using the cotton swab, gently rub the ointment into your skin. If you apply a thick layer over a small area, cover it with an adhesive strip.

MORE ABOUT
MANGOSTEEN ANALGESIC OINTMENT:

Reapply Mangosteen Analgesic Ointment as often as you like. You don't have to wipe off previous coats of the ointment, simply apply more over what's already there.

Mangosteen Analgesic Ointment will stay fresh in an airtight container outside the refrigerator for a few days if you keep it in a cool, dark place. Leave it in a convenient location if you plan to use it several times a day. If you use it sporadically, keep it in the refrigerator.

Mangosteen Analgesic Ointment will feel a little sticky on the skin. If this bothers you, try adding more lotion to the formula, although doing so will dilute its strength.

Mangosteen Analgesic Ointment is purple and may temporarily slightly discolor very fair skin. However, if you use only a little and rub it in, it can appear almost invisible.

If the Smooth Mangosteen Paste you've used to make the Analgesic Ointment has any tiny particles of rind in it, they will appear as tiny purple specks on your skin when you rub the ointment in. Once the ointment dries, it is easy to brush them off with a tissue or your fingertips.

Mangosteen Analgesic Ointment is a wonderful application for patches of rough, dry skin, especially those on the feet, hands and fingers. You may notice a difference in these areas moments after the Analgesic Ointment is applied.

37.
Mangosteen Clay

This formula acts like a sponge for pain, toxins and malaise.

TRY MIXING MANGOSTEEN WITH CLAY FOR:

- Abscesses.
- Acne.
- Arthritis.
- Fever.
- Headaches.
- Heart conditions.
- Heavy metal poisoning.
- Injuries (where the skin has not broken, or after it has healed).
- Lung conditions.
- Scars.
- Swelling.
- Tumors.
- Plus, areas where surgery has been performed—after the skin has healed.

HOW TO MIX MANGOSTEEN WITH CLAY:

1. Measure two tablespoonfuls (one ounce) of powdered clay and put it into a teacup or small bowl.

2. Add one ounce plus one teaspoonful of mangosteen. (Remember to shake the bottle before measuring, to thoroughly mix the rind particles with the rest of the juice.)

3. Thoroughly mix the ingredients together into a paste using a non-metal spoon. A plastic spoon or wooden chopsticks work fine.

MORE ABOUT MIXING MANGOSTEEN WITH CLAY:

The exact amount of mangosteen you need per two tablespoonfuls of clay depends on the kind of clay you are using, how powdery it is and how much moisture it contains. I use powered bentonite clay, and find that I need a little more than one ounce of mangosteen, which is why I suggest the extra teaspoonful. The mangosteen-clay mixture should not be runny, nor should it be so dry that you can't mix it. It should be of a consistency that allows you to apply it to your body without it dripping off. Yet it should be moist enough to stay in place. If it is too dry, it will not stick to your skin.

The amount of ingredients suggested in the recipe above can be doubled if necessary, or halved, according to the size of the area you want to treat. The amount suggested is ideal for organs, joints and tumors. If you feel you've made too much, keep the leftover mangosteen-clay in the refrigerator as it gets moldy quickly. A few hours before you want to use it next, take it out of the refrigerator so that it can warm to room temperature.

Several kinds of dried clay are available in health food stores. Choose the least expensive for topical applications. Dried clay can also be bought from ceramics supplies stores. Ask for "virgin" clay—clay that has not undergone any treatment since it was extracted from the quarry. Use a plastic or wooden spoon to mix the mangosteen and clay. Metal can interfere with the charged particles in the clay, thus making the treatment less effective.*

HOW TO USE MANGOSTEEN CLAY:
METHOD #1:

1. Identify the area you want to treat.

2. Using a wooden or plastic spoon, apply enough mangosteen-clay to cover the chosen area. Use the back of the spoon to smooth the mixture to a relatively even thickness.

---

* Dextreit, Raymond and Abehsera, Michel, *Our Earth Our Cure*, (New York, NY: Swan House Publishing), 1979, p. 17.

3. When you are finished with the treatment, use a spoon to scrape off as much of the Mangosteen Clay as you can, and throw it away. Wipe the area with a damp cloth, or wash off the remaining Mangosteen Clay in the shower.

METHOD #2:

1. Identify the area you want to treat.

2. Cut a single layer of cheesecloth large enough to cover the chosen area, plus about four inches. Center the cheesecloth on the area to be treated.

3. Using a wooden or plastic spoon, spread enough mangosteen-clay over the cheesecloth to cover the chosen area. Leave about two inches of cheesecloth around all the edges. Use the back of the spoon to smooth the Mangosteen Clay to a relatively even thickness. Despite the cheesecloth, the mixture should stick to your skin.

4. Cover the Mangosteen Clay with a layer or two of cheesecloth.

5. When you are finished with the treatment, remove the poultice by lifting the cheesecloth by the edges. Throw it in the trash. Wipe up the Mangosteen Clay that remains on the area with a damp cloth.

Method 1 is easier to do. But it is harder to remove the Mangosteen Clay and you may need to take a shower to remove it completely.

Method 2 is preferred when you want to remove the Mangosteen Clay quickly and with minimal clean-up. It would be better to use this method with children.

Here are some ideas for using Mangosteen Clay:

- For headaches, apply Mangosteen Clay to the nape of the neck and the forehead or temples.
- For fever, apply Mangosteen Clay to the lower abdomen. Remove the clay when it becomes warm.*

---

* Raymond Dextreit and Michel Abehsera, p. 20.

- For arthritis, apply Mangosteen Clay to the afflicted area to draw out the toxins and metabolic wastes that have pooled around the joints causing inflammation and pain.
- To help rid the mouth of mercury and other heavy metals, spread Mangosteen Clay on the cheeks and/or neck. This can also serve as a facial and do wonders for your skin. Follow with a favorite moisturizer.
- For sinusitis, try Mangosteen Clay on the forehead and upper cheeks. Also apply the mixture over the liver.

MORE ABOUT USING MANGOSTEEN CLAY:

The Mangosteen Clay should cover the affected area, plus some surrounding area. In general, the deeper inside the body the condition lies, and the more serious the condition, the thicker the Mangosteen Clay should be.

If rashes, eruptions or itching occurs during a Mangosteen Clay application, remove the Mangosteen Clay immediately. These symptoms can occur underneath the clay or around the edges, especially as the clay starts to dry. These effects are likely the result of toxins being pulled from inside the body, which are attracted by the clay.

Mangosteen Clay applications can be left in place for a few minutes to several hours. When the clay dries, its effectiveness diminishes so remove the mangosteen-clay at that time, if not beforehand. The process of drawing out toxins and excesses from the body seems to correlate with the clay drying out. If allowed to dry, the clay can flake off your skin and make a mess.

If you've been using Mangosteen Clay with success, you may want to try wearing it overnight. In this case, you will need to cover it to protect the bed linens. Try plastic wrap and an old towel. The plastic will keep the clay moist.

Mangosteen Clay can be applied daily. But if the application eases pain, apply it more frequently.

Section 2: Topical Applications

38.

Mangosteen for Cuticle Care

Mangosteen's exfoliating properties work very well for cuticles.

USE THE MANGOSTEEN CUTICLE CARE PROCEDURE FOR:

- Nail fungus.
- Nail infections.
- Unhealthy, dry, overgrown or unsightly cuticles.

HOW TO USE MANGOSTEEN FOR CUTICLE CARE:

1. Prepare a batch of Mangosteen Paste (page 173).

2. Spread a relatively thick layer of Mangosteen Paste over the cuticles you want to treat.

3. Gently rub the Mangosteen Paste over each cuticle at least once.

4. Keep the paste on your cuticles for about five to fifteen minutes. Then wash the paste off. Your cuticles should look noticeably better.

5. Follow with a moisturizing lotion such as Mangosteen Hand and Body Lotion (page 161).

MORE ABOUT USING MANGOSTEEN FOR CUTICLE CARE:

Use Mangosteen Hand and Body Lotion (page 161) on your cuticles daily. You could also try the formula used in the Mangosteen Sunburn Treatment (page 191), which is also very good for the skin.

If you want to treat your cuticles but don't have time to make Mangosteen Paste, try the Mangosteen Nail Treatment on page 171. However, if you have nail infections or fungus, this Cuticle Care procedure should be more effective because Mangosteen Paste is so concentrated.

For a relatively serious condition, generously cover the infected area with the Mangosteen Paste. Leave the Paste in place for as long as possible, covering it with an adhesive strip so that you can go about your daily business.

Section 2: Topical Applications

39.

Mangosteen Deodorant

For those who need an alternative to commercial products.

THE MANGOSTEEN DEODORANT CAN BE HELPFUL FOR:

- Both men and women.
- Daily personal hygiene.
- Individuals with chemical sensitivity who need an alternative to commercial deodorant and antiperspirant products.

HOW TO MAKE MANGOSTEEN DEODORANT:

1. Turn a sealed bottle of mangosteen upside down and shake it gently until the pulp and rind particles are well mixed with the rest of the juice.

2. Pour about one ounce of mangosteen into a medicine cup.

3. Wait about a minute for the rind particles to sink to the bottom of the medicine cup.

4. Carefully measure one teaspoonful of the rind-free mangosteen from the top of the medicine cup. Pour this one teaspoonful into a small resealable container.

5. Drink what is left of the ounce of mangosteen you originally poured. Count what you drink as part of your total daily dosage of mangosteen.

6. Measure a heaping teaspoonful of body lotion. Using a cotton swab, wipe the lotion off the measuring spoon and into the one teaspoonful of mangosteen. Use the cotton swab to mix the lotion and the mangosteen together. Mix well. You have now made Mangosteen Deodorant.

HOW TO APPLY MANGOSTEEN DEODORANT:

1. Dip a fingertip into the mangosteen-lotion mixture and apply it on your underarm.

2. Gently rub the mangosteen-lotion mixture into your skin until it is absorbed.

3. Apply more as needed to cover the area. Use extra if you think you will need it.

4. Repeat these steps for the other underarm.

An Alternative Method: When you're in a hurry and need some deodorant protection, simply spread a few drops mangosteen juice on your underarms. Use drops from one of your regular daily doses of mangosteen. Avoid using the mangosteen rind particles.

MORE ABOUT MANGOSTEEN DEODORANT:

The above recipe makes enough mangosteen-lotion mixture for several days. Store it in an air-tight container in a dark place away from heat, such as inside a medicine cabinet.

If you are chemically sensitive to commercial deodorants, you may also be sensitive to fragrances. Be sure to use an unscented lotion. However, use a scented lotion if you prefer, or regulate the fragrance using some unscented and some scented lotion. Even if you use unscented lotion, Mangosteen Deodorant will have the slight fruity fragrance of mangosteen juice.

Mangosteen Deodorant helps to mask odors; it is not an "antiperspirant" which inhibits the skin from perspiring. Therefore if you sweat a great deal, you may need extra applications during the day. Body odor is often a result of toxins being expelled from the body. Be sure to drink plenty of water to flush them through the kidneys instead. You might also try the Mangosteen Fast #2 (page 89) or the Mangosteen Detoxification program (page 93) to hasten detoxification.

65 Ways to Use Mangosteen

Section 2: Topical Applications

40.

Mangosteen Exfoliating Lotion

A mixture of Mangosteen Paste and your favorite moisturizing lotion makes a product with some unique applications.

TRY MANGOSTEEN EXFOLIATING LOTION FOR:

- A facial mask for conditions such as acne, aging skin, blotchy skin or pimples.
- Skin conditions, especially those characterized by dry and scaly skin.
- To soften and remove calluses on the hands and feet.

HOW TO MAKE MANGOSTEEN EXFOLIATING LOTION:

1. Put about one teaspoonful of Mangosteen Paste (page 173) into a small jar or plastic container.

2. Add approximately two teaspoonfuls of your favorite skin lotion.

3. Mix the Mangosteen Paste and the skin lotion together with a cotton swab. Mix well. You will have made a purple lotion with dark-purple flecks, which are the pieces of mangosteen rind.

Note: An alternative formula is to mix leftover mangosteen rind pieces (page 101) to facial cleansing lotion. This mixture will give you the exfoliating properties of mangosteen rind plus the cleansing properties of your lotion.

HOW TO APPLY MANGOSTEEN EXFOLIATING LOTION

How to Apply Mangosteen Exfoliating Lotion as a Facial Mask:

1. Spread a thin layer of Mangosteen Exfoliating Lotion over your face.

2. Leave it on for a few minutes until the lotion starts to dry.

3. Then gently rub the lotion around your face. The gritty mangosteen rind will exfoliate dead and dry skin.

4. Moisten a facecloth with hot tap water. Wring it out slightly and press the wet cloth against your face. This will not only feel wonderful, but it will encourage the mangosteen healing compounds to penetrate your skin. (This way, these compounds will continue to work on your skin even after you have rinsed off the lotion.) Rinse the cloth, rewet it with hot water, and reapply it to your face a few times until all traces of the lotion are wiped off. Follow with a face moisturizer.

Note: This procedure can redden your skin so use the mangosteen facial mask at night before bed.

How to Apply Mangosteen Exfoliating Lotion for skin conditions, especially dry and scaly skin on areas of the body other than the face:

1. Spread a thin layer of Mangosteen Exfoliating Lotion over the area you would like to treat.

2. Leave it uncovered or covered. However, you should cover it (plastic wrap is ideal) if you plan to move around, so that it doesn't get wiped off on your clothing or furniture.

3. Leave the lotion in place for at least an hour or overnight. Remove the lotion with a wet washcloth, or under running water in the sink or shower.

How to apply Mangosteen Exfoliating Lotion to soften and remove calluses on the hands and feet:

1. Spread some Mangosteen Exfoliating Lotion over the calluses you want to treat. To see for yourself how effective this application can be, treat only one hand or foot at a time so that you can compare the results with untreated areas.

2. Cover the area with plastic wrap so that you can move around without the Mangosteen Exfoliating Lotion rubbing off. Or insert the treated hand or foot into a large, plastic, food-storage bag.

3. After about fifteen to thirty minutes, remove the plastic.

4. Use a luffa sponge, nail brush, pumice stone or dry facecloth to rub the treated calluses. Sit on the edge of an empty bathtub to do this, because flakes of dried lotion and old skin will be rubbed off. Rubbing allows the mangosteen rind pieces to exfoliate the hardened skin. Ideally, continue to rub until all the pieces of rind are off your skin. Wipe the area with a damp washcloth.

MORE ABOUT MANGOSTEEN EXFOLIATING LOTION:

Adding lotion to Mangosteen Paste gives it a moisturizing effect, which can be particularly helpful for patches of dry, itchy and scaly skin. As an added benefit, these moisturizing ingredients, which are designed to soak into the skin, help mangosteen's healing compounds penetrate the skin as well.

Mangosteen Exfoliating Lotion has a gritty texture, which is due to the pieces of mangosteen rind. Be sure to shake the bottle of mangosteen very well before you pour some to make Mangosteen Paste (page 173). This way, you will have as many of the rind particles as possible.

If you have mixed Mangosteen Paste with a moisturizing lotion that contains preservatives, you can store the resulting Mangosteen Exfoliating Lotion at room temperature for several days. Keep it in a well-sealed container, in a cool, dark place. Otherwise, keep it in the refrigerator.

41.

Mangosteen Eye Poultice

A mangosteen poultice placed over the eyes can be helpful for a variety of eye conditions as well as headaches.

TRY THE MANGOSTEEN EYE POULTICE FOR:

- Eyestrain.
- Tired eyes.
- Headaches.
- Stress.
- Pink eye.
- Eye infections.
- Eyelid infections.
- Inflammation of the eyelid.

HOW TO MAKE AND APPLY A MANGOSTEEN EYE POULTICE:

1. Turn a sealed bottle of mangosteen upside down and shake it until the mangosteen pulp and rind particles are well mixed throughout the juice. Pour one ounce of mangosteen into a medicine cup. Wait for the pulp and rind particles to settle.

2. Carefully measure one teaspoonful of particle-free mangosteen from the top of the medicine cup. Pour this onto a dinner plate or cereal bowl.

3. Drink the remaining mangosteen as part of your daily dosage of mangosteen. Do the Oral Detox Procedure with at least one sip. This will help mangosteen's healing compounds to reach the eyes from the inside.

4. Measure one tablespoonful (which equals three teaspoonsfuls) of hot water. Add it to the one teaspoonful of mangosteen and stir the liquids together.

5. Fold a paper towel in half lengthwise two times. You will end up with a long, thin rectangle.

6. Hold the short ends of the rectangle and dip the center of it into the mangosteen-water mixture. Wet only the centermost five or six inches. The liquid will gradually spread to the dry ends.

7. Lie down, close your eyes, and place the center of the wet paper towel over the bridge of your nose. Gently press the paper towel over your eyeballs and into the corners of your eyes, to conform the Eye Poultice to the contours of your face.

8. Rest with the Eye Poultice in place for twenty to thirty minutes.

MORE ABOUT THE MANGOSTEEN EYE POULTICE:

The Mangosteen Eye Poultice can be very soothing and relaxing. If used regularly, it may prevent headaches due to eyestrain. If you prefer to lie on your side, place a towel beneath your head so the mangosteen doesn't stain your pillow. The Eye Poultice will naturally adhere to your skin, just enough to allow you some range of movement.

Try to avoid getting the mangosteen juice in your eyes, as any remaining particles of pulp or rind can irritate them.

The ratio of mangosteen to water in this formula is one part mangosteen to three parts water. You could vary this ratio if you wanted to. I chose it because it made the Eye Poultice more economical, yet the formula gives you enough total volume of liquid to wet the paper towel. Moreover, undiluted mangosteen can redden or irritate sensitive skin, such as that of the face and eyelids. Adding water also reduces the possibility that some mangosteen pulp or rind pieces get inside the eye, which could be very irritating, too.

The Eye Poultice can also be used specifically for headaches. Wet the entire folded paper towel with the mangosteen-water mixture. Center the poultice on your forehead and press the ends on your temples. Put an old towel beneath your head to prevent any drips of mangosteen-water from staining your pillow.

If you are treating only one eye, adjust the size of the paper towel. Simply fold it to the desired size.

Section 2: Topical Applications

42.

Mangosteen First Aid for Minor Wounds

The information in this chapter is meant to supplement—not replace—standard first aid procedures.

When treating emergency situations, even minor ones, it is essential to use common sense and call upon the help of an Emergency Medical Team if necessary.

MANGOSTEEN CAN BE HELPFUL FOR:

- Abrasions and scrapes.
- Bee stings and insect bites.
- Blows and bruises.
- Burns.
- Cuts and other small wounds.

HOW TO USE MANGOSTEEN FOR ABRASIONS AND SCRAPES:

Abrasions and scrapes are relatively superficial wounds, which don't usually produce a significant amount of bleeding. Use a cotton ball soaked in mangosteen to help clean the area of any dirt and debris. Use just the liquid part of the mangosteen juice. Do this by shaking the mangosteen bottle as usual, pouring out about one ounce, letting the rind particles settle to the bottom of the container and then dipping the cotton just in the top portion of the dose. (Have the injured person drink the leftover mangosteen that you don't apply topically.) However for emergency situations, you may not want to spend the time separating the rind from the rest of the juice. Simply take the bottle from the refrigerator and pour a dose without shaking the bottle. You could also cleanse the wound with a mixture of mangosteen and water, in approximately equal amounts.

After cleansing the wound, decide if it should be air-dried or covered. If you want the wound to air-dry, leave it alone at this point. The mangosteen that you applied when cleansing the abrasion will supply antiseptic healing compounds to the area. If the abrasion or scrape needs more antiseptic protection, apply a Mangosteen Mini-Poultice (page 169) for small areas. For larger areas, try the Mangosteen Poultice (page 179) or Mangosteen Rash Plaster (page 183). Cover the mangosteen application with an adhesive strip (for small areas) or gauze and first aid tape (for larger areas).

HOW TO USE MANGOSTEEN FOR BEE STINGS AND INSECT BITES:

1. Soak a cotton ball in Mangosteen and place it on the sting. If the sting is painful or if the victim is distressed or upset, give him or her a Trauma Dose (page 57).

2. When the cotton ball warms from body heat, soak another cotton ball in more mangosteen juice and reapply. Do this as often as needed. The cold temperature of a fresh cotton ball soaked in refrigerated mangosteen offers an analgesic effect of its own.

3. Finally, replace the cotton once again, this time using a small enough piece to fit beneath an adhesive strip. Wet only half the cotton, so it doesn't leak and stain clothing.

4. Secure the cotton in place with an adhesive strip or a piece of first aid tape.

HOW TO USE MANGOSTEEN FOR BLOWS AND BRUISES:

Bruises involve internal bleeding, which causes discoloration on the skin. Apply a Mangosteen Poultice (page 179) or a poultice made with Mangosteen Astringent (page 127) as soon as possible over the hurt area. You could also try Mangosteen Paste (page 173), which you would then cover with an adhesive strip or a gauze pad and first aid tape.

If the newly bruised area is painful and swollen, apply an ice pack over the Mangosteen Poultice. The ice will provide an analgesic effect of its own. Both mangosteen and cold packs help reduce swelling and inflammation.

Old, painful bruises seem to respond better to heat packs, as from a hot, moist towel or hot water bottle. Place a heat pack over a Mangosteen Poultice or Mangosteen Paste that has been covered with gauze or plastic wrap. Heat also helps mangosteen's healing compounds to be absorbed into the body, thereby helping the body heal.

HOW TO USE MANGOSTEEN FOR MINOR BURNS:

For relatively minor burns, apply mangosteen generously to the area for about thirty minutes. Severe burns should be treated by emergency medical professionals.

If the burn is on a finger, pour some mangosteen into a cup and submerge the burned area. For burns in other areas, cover the burn with a cotton ball soaked in mangosteen. The cotton should be dripping wet, so apply it over a protected surface so the mangosteen does not stain. As soon as the cotton warms from body heat, replace it with another one soaked in mangosteen. For larger burns, instead of cotton balls, use a single layer of paper towel or gauze soaked in mangosteen.

HOW TO USE MANGOSTEEN FOR MINOR CUTS:

1. Clean the wound by placing it under running water. Then apply pressure to help stop the bleeding. Asses how serious the wound is, what other injuries may be present, and if you need to call for help. Try to calm the one who has been injured.

2. Make a quick Mangosteen Poultice by pouring some mangosteen directly onto the cloth or paper towel that you are using to apply pressure to the wound. Don't bother shaking the bottle to mix the pulp and rind with the rest of the juice. As this is an emergency situation, you'll want the mangosteen on the wound as soon as possible. The mangosteen will help the wound stop bleeding.

3. Give the victim a Trauma Dose (page 57) and then have him or her take an Auto-Distribution Dose (page 201) with at least one sip.

4. After the cut has stopped bleeding, cover it with a Mangosteen Mini-Poultice (page 169) or Mangosteen Poultice (page 179). Which application you use would depend on the size of the injury.

MORE ABOUT USING MANGOSTEEN AS FIRST AID:

Remember to follow standard first aid procedures and call for help if necessary.

Take a Mangosteen Trauma Dose (page 57) as soon as possible after first aid has been applied. This will give your body a rich supply of healing compounds to aid the healing process. Be sure to do the Auto-Distribution Procedure (page 201) with at least one sip of your Trauma Dose. This will get mangosteen's healing energy to the areas that need it as soon as possible.

Mangosteen is an excellent first aid tool because of its ability to promote healing, reduce inflammation, curtail infection and stop bleeding.

Section 2: Topical Applications

43.
Mangosteen Foot Treatment

Here is a fantastic treatment for your feet. If you cannot reach your feet, you will need someone to help you perform this procedure.

TRY THE MANGOSTEEN FOOT TREATMENT FOR:

- Arthritis.
- Athlete's foot.
- Blisters.
- Calluses.
- Dry skin.
- Foot pain.
- Fungus.
- Itchy feet.

HOW TO APPLY THE MANGOSTEEN FOOT TREATMENT:

1. Gently shake a sealed bottle of mangosteen upside down until the rind particles are well mixed throughout the juice.

2. Measure one teaspoonful and pour it into a medicine cup.

3. Measure one-half teaspoonful of olive oil and add it to the mangosteen.

4. Measure one-half teaspoonful of your favorite moisturizing lotion. Use a cotton swab to remove the lotion from the measuring spoon and put it into the medicine cup with the mangosteen.

5. Use the same cotton swab to stir the ingredients together. Mix well. You will have made the formula for the Mangosteen Foot Treatment, and will have two teaspoonfuls of mangosteen-oil-lotion mixture.

6. Before bedtime, or when you plan to be off your feet for at least an hour, sit down with the Foot Treatment formula and an old pair of socks. Use a cotton swab or your fingers to pour half the mixture, about one teaspoonful, onto one foot. Spread the mixture around your foot using your fingertips or a cotton ball. Put some between each of your toes and under your toe nails. Apply extra on problem areas.

7. Put one of the old socks on your foot.

8. Repeat Steps 6 and 7 with your other foot.

MORE ABOUT THE MANGOSTEEN FOOT TREATMENT:

Ideally, before you put on each sock, wait at least a minute for the Mangosteen Foot Treatment formula to soak in. It will take more than a minute to completely soak in (but who has the time to wait any longer?) hence we use the socks to keep the formula in place so that we can put our attention elsewhere.

After applying the formula to your feet, you will have extra on your fingertips. Apply this to your arms and elbows, or wherever else on your body you'd like to put it. It may feel sticky until it dries. You may prefer to wipe your fingertips on a paper towel before putting on each sock.

Keep the socks on for at least an hour or until morning. It's okay to get up and walk around. The socks will keep the lotion on your feet and protect the carpet. However, the lotion will stain your socks, so use old ones or dark-colored ones.

When you remove the socks, the mangosteen-oil-lotion mixture will have completely soaked in, so no need to rinse the formula off your feet. Your feet should feel remarkably softer and more smooth.

While wearing the formula on your feet, mangosteen's healing compounds will penetrate your skin. Its anti-inflammatory properties can ease the pain of arthritis and the irritation of skin conditions, plus its anti-fungal properties can ease athlete's foot and other fungal infections. Several daily applications may be necessary. Perform this treatment as often as you like.

Section 2: Topical Applications

44.

Mangosteen Hand and Body Lotion

A skin softener and mild therapeutic agent for skin conditions.

TRY MANGOSTEEN HAND AND BODY LOTION FOR A VARIETY OF SKIN CONDITIONS INCLUDING:

- Dermatitis.
- Dry skin.
- Rashes.
- Rough, calloused skin.
- As a daily moisturizing lotion for the hands, face and body.

HOW TO MAKE AND APPLY MANGOSTEEN HAND AND BODY LOTION:

1. Shake a sealed bottle of mangosteen, held upside down, until the rind particles are well mixed throughout the juice.

2. Pour a one-ounce dose into a medicine cup. Wait a few minutes for the rind particles to settle to the bottom of the medicine cup.

3. Use a one-half teaspoon measuring spoon to scoop up some particle-free mangosteen from the top of the medicine cup. Pour this into a small plastic container. Drink the remaining mangosteen juice as one of your daily doses of mangosteen.

4. Squeeze some of your favorite skin lotion into a one-tablespoon measuring spoon. Use a cotton swab to wipe the lotion out of the measuring spoon and into the container holding the one-half teaspoonful of mangosteen. Use the same cotton swab to mix the lotion and mangosteen together. Mix well. You have now made Mangosteen Hand and Body Lotion.

5. Using the cotton swab, or your fingertips, spread some of the Mangosteen Hand and Body Lotion on your face, hands, elbows, arms, legs and feet, or wherever treatment is needed. Gently rub the Mangosteen Lotion into your skin. It may take a minute or two for the lotion to soak in.

MORE ABOUT MANGOSTEEN HAND AND BODY LOTION:

I've experimented with many ratios of mangosteen and body lotion to find a formula that contained as much mangosteen as possible without feeling sticky when applied on the skin. As different brands of body lotions have different ingredients, some may produce a formula that leaves the skin feeling more sticky than others. So, you may need to vary the ratio of mangosteen and lotion until you find your preference. For example, if you find that the Mangosteen Lotion still feels sticky after it soaks in and dries, then add more lotion. If you'd like a more therapeutic application for skin conditions, use more mangosteen. Or, add Smooth Mangosteen Paste (page 177).

Mangosteen Lotion may be preferred over the Rash Plaster (page 183) for babies and those with sensitive skin. If you use this formula for rashes, dermatitis or other skin conditions you may prefer using a body lotion that is unscented and that contains natural ingredients.

Section 2: Topical Applications

45.

Mangosteen Hemorrhoid Treatments

Try one of these procedures for relief…

THESE TREATMENTS MAY BE USED FOR:

- Hemorrhoids.
- And other conditions including burning, itching and irritated anal tissue.

HOW TO DO THE MANGOSTEEN HEMORRHOID TREATMENT METHOD 1:

1. Before bedtime, pour one teaspoonful of mangosteen into a small bowl or medicine cup. (In this case, you do not have to separate out the rind particles.)

2. Press a cotton ball into the mangosteen until it soaks up all the juice. Take the bowl with you into the bedroom.

3. Spread an old towel on the mid-portion of your bed's fitted sheet to protect it from being stained by the mangosteen.

4. Get into bed and lie down on your side. Position the mangosteen-soaked cotton on the affected area. The pulpy side of the cotton ball should be against your skin. Press the cotton ball into your body, or against it, as needed.

5. Keep the cotton ball in place as you sleep.

HOW TO DO THE MANGOSTEEN HEMORRHOID TREATMENT METHOD 2:

1. Pour about one tablespoonful of mangosteen into a small bowl or medicine cup and keep it on the bathroom sink. Each time you are finished visiting the bathroom, do the following steps:

2. Dip a clean cotton ball or a cotton swab into the mangosteen. The cotton should be wet but not dripping wet.

3. Sit on the toilet. Wipe the affected area with the cotton ball or cotton swab. Or press the cotton against the area for several seconds.

MORE ABOUT THE MANGOSTEEN HEMORRHOID TREATMENTS:

The anti-inflammatory effect of mangosteen can ease swelling and irritation in the affected area. So expect some relief on the first application. However, to achieve and maintain comfort, constant contact between mangosteen and the affected area may be required as in Method 1. The mangosteen would then have time to soak into the skin and reach deeper layers of tissue.

During the day, you may need to repeat Method 2 every few minutes and then gradually less often. If you feel better with the cotton in place, but need to go about your day, try pressing the cotton against your body as in Method 1. Then stand up carefully to see how well the cotton stays in place. It will depend on your body shape. Also, the more walking you need to do, the less likely the cotton ball will stay in place. Use a panty liner in your underwear to prevent the mangosteen from staining your clothes.

Section 2: Topical Applications

You don't have to worry if some mangosteen particles get soaked up by the cotton. But if they happen to be irritating because of their hard, particulate nature, let them settle to the bottom of the medicine cup before dipping in your cotton ball.

A cotton ball made of pure cotton is preferable to "cosmetic puffs" which look like cotton balls but are made of synthetic fiber. Cotton holds more liquid than synthetic fiber. It also tends to adhere better to the skin.

Soaking the cotton in refrigerated mangosteen makes the cotton ball like a miniature cold pack, which has its own pain-relieving properties.

Section 2: Topical Applications

46.

Mangosteen Massage Oil

A mangosteen massage is a real treat!

TRY A MANGOSTEEN MASSAGE FOR:

- Illness.
- Low vitality.
- Muscle cramps.
- Sore and painful muscles.
- Stress.

HOW TO MAKE MANGOSTEEN MASSAGE OIL:

1. Pour one tablespoonful of your favorite unscented massage oil into a container such as a bowl, cup or plastic bottle. (Jojoba oil or light olive oil is particularly nice.)

2. Shake a sealed bottle of mangosteen upside down until the pulp and rind particles are mixed throughout the juice. Pour a one-ounce dose into a medicine cup.

3. Wait a few minutes for the rind particles to settle. Carefully pour the particle-free top portion of the mangosteen juice into the tablespoon. Medicine cups are great for this, as you can squeeze them as you pour the juice and thereby control the

amount you pour. It's okay if some of the pulp is poured into the tablespoon, but if you notice any particles, pour the mangosteen back into the medicine cup and repeat this Step. Next time try pouring one teaspoonful at a time (three teaspoonfuls equal one tablespoonful).

4. Mix the oil and mangosteen together with your finger. Or, if you have added the oil and juice to a bottle, shake the bottle. Shaking will produce the best emulsion.

5. Apply Mangosteen Massage Oil as you would any massage oil.

MORE ABOUT MANGOSTEEN MASSAGE OIL:

While doing the massage, if the mangosteen-oil mixture feels too sticky then add a bit more oil. As the Mangosteen Massage Oil soaks in and dries, the sticky feeling will go away.

The mangosteen-oil mixture separates quickly. Remix it each time you apply more to the body. If you plan to use up the mixture within a few days, it need not be refrigerated.

Expect muscle tension and stress to be relieved more quickly when incorporating mangosteen into a massage. Mangosteen Massage Oil can also have a therapeutic effect on skin conditions and makes the skin feel wonderfully soft.

A massage therapist's hands will also appreciate Mangosteen Massage Oil, not only because of the skin-softening effect, but also because they won't tire as quickly.

Enhance the benefits of Mangosteen Massage by offering the person who will receive the massage an ounce of mangosteen to drink before the massage begins. Drinking mangosteen enhances the beneficial effects of mangosteen applied topically.

Section 2: Topical Applications

47.

Mangosteen Mini-Poultice

An easy poultice for the smallest needs.

TRY THE MANGOSTEEN MINI-POULTICE FOR CONDITIONS SUCH AS:

- Acne and pimples.
- Bee stings.
- Boils and abscesses.
- Bruises.
- Infected pierced earring holes.
- Insect bites.
- Irritated or infected moles.
- Puncture wounds.
- Ringworm.
- Small scars.
- Warts.

HOW TO MAKE AND APPLY THE MANGOSTEEN MINI-POULTICE:

1. Prepare a poultice pad by tearing off a piece of a cotton ball. The piece should be large enough to cover the area you want to treat. If the area is relatively large or particularly painful, use a whole cotton ball.

2. Turn a sealed bottle of mangosteen upside down and shake it gently until the pulp and rind particles are mixed throughout the juice.

3. Pour a small amount of mangosteen into a bowl—about one-half teaspoonful.

4. Press the flattened cotton into the mangosteen. Gently squeeze out any excess. The cotton should be wet but not dripping.

5. Place the flat wet cotton over the target area.

6. The surface tension of the wet cotton may be enough to keep it attached to your skin if you move around carefully. If the target area is underneath clothing, or if you are particularly active, or if you are putting the Mini-Poultice on a child, secure the cotton with first-aid tape or an adhesive bandage.

MORE ABOUT THE MANGOSTEEN MINI-POULTICE:

A variation is to keep the cotton ball somewhat round and wet only half of it. Apply the wet side against the skin. The dry portion of the cotton will soak up the excess liquid so it won't drip. However, the poultice is less likely to stay in place by itself and will need to be secured to the body.

If you are using the Mini-Poultice as first aid for an insect bite or wound, simply grab a napkin or paper towel and tear off a piece, quickly dip it in some mangosteen and apply to the area in need. Then prepare a cotton ball as described above. Cotton holds more mangosteen than a layer or two of paper towel, and so it is preferred.

Chronic conditions such as warts and small scars will require daily treatment. Try applying the Mini-Poultice on these areas every night before bed. Acute conditions such as insect bites may require only one or two applications.

As with the larger Mangosteen Poultice (page 179), the Mini-Poultice brings mangosteen's healing compounds to the skin as well as increases the blood supply there to support healing. The anti-histiminic properties of mangosteen bring pain relief to insect bites and its antiseptic properties fight infection.

Section 2: Topical Applications

48.

Mangosteen Nail Treatment

This procedure may be done on a single nail, all the fingernails, or the toenails.

TRY THE MANGOSTEEN NAIL TREATMENT FOR:

- Brittle and broken nails.
- Unhealthy cuticles.
- Infected hag nails.
- Unhealthy cuticles.

HOW TO APPLY THE MANGOSTEEN NAIL TREATMENT:

1. Turn a sealed bottle of mangosteen upside down and shake it gently until the pulp and rind particles are well mixed throughout the juice.

2. Pour one or two teaspoonfuls of mangosteen into a bowl. (It's OK to include the rind particles in this treatment.)

3. Tear a cotton ball into pieces large enough to cover each of the nails you want to treat.

4. Dip one side of a cotton piece into the mangosteen. It should be only half wet. The dry part will soak up the excess juice, so it won't drip.

5. Place the wet side of the cotton on a nail to cover it. Press gently to help adhere the wet cotton to your nail.

6. Repeat Steps 4 and 5 for the other nails you want to treat.

7. While the cotton is in place, massage each nail by squeezing it several times between the thumb and forefinger of the opposite hand. This will improve circulation to the nail, and enhance the benefits of the therapy. It will also help keep your fingers warm.

MORE ABOUT THE MANGOSTEEN NAIL TREATMENT:

Keep the cotton in place for fifteen to thirty minutes. It's a good treatment to do while you're watching television or reading. For general nail care, do the Mangosteen Nail Treatment every week or two, or every time you cut your nails. If a nail problem is serious or painful, do the Mangosteen Nail Treatment daily. Meanwhile, make a batch of Mangosteen Paste (page 173) and then do the Mangosteen Cuticle Care procedure (page 139) which is a more powerful therapy.

If you have just used nail polish remover, wash your hands well with soap before applying the Mangosteen Nail Treatment so that the chemicals of the nail polish do not interfere with the mangosteen.

If you do this treatment while you are resting, the surface tension of the wet cotton may be enough to keep the cotton pieces in place. But if you want to move around, secure the cotton to your nail with first-aid tape.

49.

Mangosteen Paste

Mangosteen Paste offers a high concentration of mangosteen healing compounds.

TRY MANGOSTEEN PASTE FOR CONDITIONS IN RELATIVELY SMALL, DEFINABLE AREAS, SUCH AS:

- Acne.
- Arthritis.
- Athletic injuries.
- Blisters.
- Boils
- Bruises.
- Canker sores.
- Carpal Tunnel Syndrome.
- Fungal infections.
- Gum conditions such as infection and gingivitis.
- Inflammation.
- Mosquito bites.
- Nail cuticles that are infected, damaged or unsightly.
- Sore throat.
- Swelling.
- Topical infections.
- Tumors.

HOW TO MAKE MANGOSTEEN PASTE:

1. Turn a sealed bottle of mangosteen upside down and shake it gently until the pulp and rind are thoroughly mixed with the juice.

2. Pour an ounce of mangosteen onto a dinner plate. (Make sure the dinner plate has a deep enough indentation in the center that the liquid won't spill off. Most dinner plates should be just fine.)

3. Put the plate where you can keep an eye on it. Over time, the water in the juice will evaporate and the mangosteen will thicken. Stir the mangosteen every few hours to maintain a uniform consistency because the mangosteen at the edges of the plate will dry out faster. The paste is ready when you tip the plate, and the mangosteen stays in place. It should have the consistency of a soft jam.

4. Use a rubber spatula to scrap the Mangosteen Paste off the plate. Put the paste into a small jar or plastic container. Store it tightly covered in the refrigerator. Saved this way, Mangosteen Paste can be stored for several weeks and used as needed.

MORE ABOUT MAKING MANGOSTEEN PASTE:

This recipe makes about a teaspoonful of Mangosteen Paste. (Exactly how much depends on how much water has evaporated.) A little Mangosteen Paste goes a long way. Most applications require only one-sixteenth to one-quarter teaspoonful of paste so you should have plenty for a few applications.

I prefer using a dinner plate instead of a bowl to make Mangosteen Paste. On a plate, more mangosteen is exposed to air. This speeds up the evaporation. Do not try to evaporate water from mangosteen by putting it on the stove. The temperature at which the water would steam away is high enough to destroy some of mangosteen's healing compounds.

Monitor the mangosteen while it is becoming Mangosteen Paste. If too much water evaporates, the dried mangosteen will resemble fruit leather. If this occurs, pour some water on the dried paste. Spread the water over the mangosteen. Soon the paste will reconstitute. If it is now too liquidy once again, leave it out again until the paste is the proper consistency.

How fast mangosteen will become Mangosteen Paste depends on the humidity in the air. In hot, dry climates or in an air-conditioned room it may take a day. In average humidity, it may take two or three days. If you live in a very humid climate, you may be unable to make Mangosteen Paste indoors. An alternative is to place mangosteen in sunlight. Doing so promotes evaporation and vitalizes the Mangosteen Paste with the sun's energy. However, in sunlight, evaporation can happen very quickly so be sure to keep a close eye on it. It would also be wise to put the mangosteen into a bowl instead of a plate. Then you can easily cover it with a wire screen to keep out insects.

HOW TO USE MANGOSTEEN PASTE:

1. Spread Mangosteen Paste over the area to be treated. In general, apply a thin layer of paste over skin conditions. For conditions inside the body, the paste layer should be thicker.

2. You can either cover the treatment area or keep it uncovered. If you plan to move around or wear the paste overnight, covering it is essential so that it doesn't rub off and stain your clothes or furniture. If the area is small, use an adhesive bandage. If it is too large for that, cover it with plastic wrap and/or gauze, then secure with first-aid tape. Using plastic wrap prevents the paste from seeping through the gauze. Ideally, keep the paste uncovered for awhile if you are treating blisters, boils, inflammation or tumors. These areas need to expel toxins or fluid. As the paste dries, it tends to draw out this excess. (See also Mangosteen Clay on page 135.)

3. Keep the paste in place for at least an hour or overnight.

MORE ABOUT USING MANGOSTEEN PASTE:

When you are finished, if the paste is still moist, remove it with a damp cloth. Wipe the area a second and third time to remove any residue that might leave your skin feeling sticky. If the paste is dry, the easiest way to remove it is under running tap water or in the shower.

The healing compounds in Mangosteen Paste are very concentrated and are readily absorbed by the body. To help the compounds enter the body more quickly, penetrate more deeply and thereby shorten treatment time, apply moist heat over the covered paste. Heating the paste is unnecessary when treating skin conditions as the mangosteen healing compounds access the skin directly.

Because of mangosteen's purple color and how concentrated Mangosteen Paste is, it may stain your skin. But this effect is short-lived, and it is more likely to occur when your skin is dry. If you do have dry skin, also try Mangosteen Hand and Body Lotion (page 161).

Newly made Mangosteen Paste will be at room temperature; stored paste will be refrigerator cold. If are going to use stored paste, you may prefer to leave it out of the refrigerator to bring it to room temperature before applying.

More ideas for using Mangosteen Paste:

- For gum conditions, tear off a piece of a cotton ball that is large enough to cover the area you want to treat. Spread Mangosteen Paste over one side of the cotton. Place the cotton inside your mouth with the Mangosteen Paste against the affected gums. (See also the Mangosteen Tooth and Gum Compress on page 221 and the Tooth and Gum Pack on page 223.)
- For mosquito bites, apply a thick layer over the bite. Cover with an adhesive strip or let air-dry.
- For sore throats, spread Mangosteen Paste on each side of the neck over points of pain as well as swollen glands. Some people will enjoy the cool feeling of the Mangosteen Paste over their sore throat. Others may find that covering the paste with a hot, moist towel is soothing and, therefore, preferred.
- To treat nail cuticles, spread a thick layer of Mangosteen Paste over them. Follow the procedure for using Mangosteen for Cuticle Care on page 139.
- For injuries, tumors or painful areas, apply a thick layer of the paste where the pain is centered.

SMOOTH MANGOSTEEN PASTE:

Smooth Mangosteen Paste is made like regular Mangosteen Paste, except that the pulp and rind particles are removed from the juice beforehand. This results in a paste that is smooth and nonabrasive when applied. Smooth Mangosteen Paste is preferred over regular Mangosteen Paste for:

- Sensitive skin or conditions where the particles might be irritating.
- Conditions where the rind particles might get stuck in the skin, such as dry, scaly skin, some dermatitis, canker sores, open acne or insect bites that have been scratched open.
- And for making Mangosteen Analgesic Ointment (page 131).

HOW TO MAKE SMOOTH MANGOSTEEN PASTE:

1. Turn a sealed bottle of mangosteen upside down and shake it gently until the pulp and rind are thoroughly mixed with the juice.

2. Pour two ounces of mangosteen. Either use two one-ounce medicine cups or a small, narrow glass such as a shot glass. Wait about a minute until the rind particles settle.

3. Pour the top, particle-free half of the juice onto a dinner plate. You should have about one ounce of mangosteen on the plate. Drink the remaining mangosteen, which is filled with pulp and rind particles, as one of your daily doses of mangosteen.

4. Continue with Step 3 of "How to Make Mangosteen Paste" (on page 174).

50.

The Mangosteen Poultice

The Mangosteen Poultice has a wider variety of uses than any other topical mangosteen application.

TRY A MANGOSTEEN POULTICE FOR CONDITIONS SUCH AS:

- Abdominal pain due to diarrhea, inflammation, ulcers and diverticulitis.
- Arthritis.
- Athletic injuries.
- Carpal Tunnel Syndrome.
- Injuries and conditions of the bones and joints.
- Lung conditions such as asthma, bronchitis and allergic responses.
- Malfunctioning organs.
- Skin conditions such as acne, dermatitis, eczema and psoriasis.
- Sprains.
- Strengthening weak joints before strenuous exercise.
- Tumors.
- And as an antiseptic and astringent over wounds and sores.

HOW TO MAKE AND
APPLY A MANGOSTEEN POULTICE:
METHOD #1:

This is the basic method for applying a Mangosteen Poultice.

1. Turn a sealed mangosteen bottle upside down then right-side up several times to disperse the rind and pulp throughout the juice.

2. Measure one tablespoonful of mangosteen and pour it onto a dinner plate.

3. Prepare a poultice pad. A three-inch or four-inch square gauze pad is ideal for most poultice applications. If you don't have gauze, a paper towel cut to size will do.

4. Press the pad into the juice. It should be wet but not dripping wet.

5. Place the poultice over the area you want to treat. Cover it with a source of moist heat. This could be a small towel that has been soaked in hot tap water and wrung out, or a hot water bottle. If you use a towel, cover the poultice first with some plastic wrap, to protect the towel from getting stained.

6. After about fifteen to thirty minutes, or when the heat source cools, remove it and throw the poultice in the trash.

METHOD #2:

With the previous method, the poultice is cold when placed on the body. This may be unimportant for some people, especially since the poultice will be warmed by the heat source soon after placement. However, cold poultices can be stressful or unpleasant for children or for those who are very weak and feeling fragile. There are several ways to heat a poultice. The easiest method I've found so far is as follows:

1. Follow Steps 1 – 4 above.

2. Prepare your heat source. Either fill a hot water bottle or heat a small towel with hot water and wring it out.

3. Place the poultice on top of the heat source. If you are using a towel, place a sheet of plastic wrap over it first. This will protect the towel from getting stained.

4. When the poultice is warm, place it on the area you want to treat. Put the heat source on top. If the heat source is too hot, put a towel between it and the poultice.

MORE ABOUT THE MANGOSTEEN POULTICE:

To treat areas inside the body, mangosteen's healing compounds must penetrate the skin. The heat provided by a hot moist towel or hot water bottle encourages this to occur. If you use a hot moist towel, wear rubber gloves to protect your hands in order get the towel hot enough. If using a hot water bottle, fill it only half-full. This way it can conform to the contours of your body and more easily stay in place over the treatment area.

Mangosteen Poultices seem to strengthen areas over which they are placed. This makes mangosteen an effective preventive measure before strenuous activity as well as a therapeutic remedy afterwards. For example, if you have a weak ankle and are planning to run a race, consider using the Mangosteen Poultice on the ankle a few times before the race begins.

Mangosteen will stain so place an old towel under the area of your body that is to receive the poultice. This will protect your clothing and furniture in case the poultice drips.

It is important to make sure that the pulp and rind are completely dispersed throughout the mangosteen before you pour a dose for making a poultice. This way, a poultice made when a mangosteen bottle is first opened will contain the same amount of pulp and rind as a poultice made when the bottle is almost empty.

Gauze pads are the best material for making Mangosteen Poultices. The open fibers in a gauze pad hold liquid just enough to contain it. The liquid is free to access the body. In contrast, the fibers of paper towels are designed to absorb and hold liquid and are, therefore, not as good for poultices. However, you may need to use paper towels if that's all you have available, or if the treatment area is relatively large. When using a paper towel, fold it no more than two layers thick.

65 Ways to Use Mangosteen

Your skin may become reddened after a Mangosteen Poultice has been applied. This occurs because of the heat and also because mangosteen can increase circulation over the area where it is placed. If your skin is dry, it may also become slightly stained by the purple mangosteen. Both the redness and staining effects are temporary.

Section 2: Topical Applications

51.

Mangosteen Rash Plaster

This treatment is used specifically for skin conditions that cover a relatively large area.

TRY A RASH PLASTER
FOR CONDITIONS INCLUDING:

- Chaffing.
- Chicken pox.
- Diaper rash.
- Eczema.
- Hives.
- Liver spots.
- Minor burns.
- Pimples and acne.
- Poison Ivy.
- Psoriasis.
- Rashes.
- Skin eruptions.
- Skin irritations.
- Sunburn.

HOW TO MAKE A
MANGOSTEEN RASH PLASTER:

1. Select a plaster cloth that will cover the area you want to treat. You could use cheesecloth, an unfolded sterile gauze pad, a piece of an old T-shirt, or simply a paper towel. A plaster cloth should be relatively thin.

2. Turn a sealed bottle of mangosteen upside down and shake it gently to thoroughly mix the pulp and rind particles with the rest of the juice.

3. Pour about one ounce of mangosteen into a medicine cup.

4. Wait about a minute for the heavier rind particles to sink to the bottom of the medicine cup.

5. Measure one tablespoonful of the rind-free mangosteen from the top of the medicine cup. Pour this into a bowl. If your plaster cloth is more than about four inches square, pour the mangosteen instead onto a dinner plate. This will make it easier to distribute the mangosteen evenly throughout the plaster cloth.

6. Drink what is left of the ounce of mangosteen you originally poured. Count this as part of your total daily dosage of mangosteen.

7. Add one tablespoonful of very hot water to the mangosteen in the bowl or plate. Gently mix the two liquids together.

HOW TO APPLY A
MANGOSTEEN RASH PLASTER:

1. Press the plaster cloth into the mangosteen-water mixture. Do not turn the cloth over.

2. Hold the cloth over the bowl so that any excess liquid drips off. Squeeze it gently if necessary. The cloth could be wet, but not dripping wet.

3. Lay the plaster cloth over the treatment area to cover it. The pulpy side of the cloth should be touching the skin. The plaster will feel cool at first, even when mixing hot water with the mangosteen. But the plaster will soon warm up with body heat.

4. Press the plaster cloth on the skin and mold it around the contours of your body. The plaster cloth will be slightly adhesive; perhaps just enough that you won't need to secure it in place.

5. Apply additional plaster cloths as needed to completely cover all the skin you want to treat. The Mangosteen Rash Plaster can cover a considerably large portion of the body if necessary.

6. If you'd like, cover the Rash Plaster with an old towel to protect your clothing.

7. Leave the plaster cloth in place until it dries. Or, if you've covered it with a towel, remove it after about thirty minutes. Then throw it in the trash.

MORE ABOUT THE MANGOSTEEN RASH PLASTER:

Reapply the Mangosteen Rash Plaster as often as needed.

This recipe omits the rind particles in mangosteen juice because they can irritate sensitive and sunburned skin when you try to wash them off. If this is not a problem for you, and you would like to obtain the therapeutic benefits of the mangosteen rind particles, then do not separate them out when preparing to make the Rash Plaster.

Water is added to mangosteen in this treatment so that it does not leave a sticky residue on your skin and also to make the treatment more economical, especially if you are treating large areas often. Feel free to add more water to the mixture.

The actual amount of mangosteen-water mixture you will need depends on the size of the area you are treating and the type of plaster cloth you are using. Some cloths absorb more liquid than others. The larger the treatment area and the more absorbent your plaster cloth, the more mangosteen you will need. Start with one tablespoonful of mangosteen and water as suggested above, and make a second dose if needed.

The anti-histiminic and anti-inflammatory effects of mangosteen's healing compounds can reduce itching and swelling. However, the Rash Plaster can also make the skin feel tingly as the mangosteen increases circulation in the area. This can redden the skin in some cases. Remove the plaster cloth if you feel this tingling or if your skin reddens. For this reason, apply the Rash Plaster only briefly on the face. Or, do the treatment at night before bed.

If your skin reddens from this treatment, it may be too strong for you. Next time, add more water to the mangosteen-water mixture.

In cases of contagious rashes, such as Poison Ivy, you may leave the Rash Plaster in place even when it dries out. This may prevent the rash from spreading. Keep the plaster wet with mangosteen to help control itching.

For treating sunburn, see also the Mangosteen Sunburn Treatment on page 191.

52.

Mangosteen Scalp Treatment

Even your scalp can benefit from mangosteen.

TRY THE MANGOSTEEN SCALP TREATMENT FOR:

- Dandruff.
- Itchy scalp.
- Eczema.
- Scalp sores.
- Skin eruptions on the scalp.

HOW TO APPLY THE MANGOSTEEN SCALP TREATMENT:

1. Turn a sealed bottle of mangosteen upside down and shake it gently until the pulp and rind particles are mixed throughout the juice.

2. Pour one ounce of mangosteen into a medicine cup. Wait a minute for the rind particles to settle. Measure one teaspoonful to one tablespoonful of particle-free mangosteen from the top of the medicine cup. Pour this into a second medicine cup. Use one teaspoonful for small areas and about one tablespoonful for larger areas. If you have no hair, or very little hair, the Mangosteen Poultice (page 179) or the Mangosteen Rash Plaster (page 183) may work better for you. Drink the leftover particle-rich mangosteen from the first medicine cup as part of your total daily dosage of mangosteen.

3. Part the hair over the section of your scalp that needs treatment. Hold the medicine cup of rind-free mangosteen over the area and pour some mangosteen on it. The mangosteen should make direct contact with your skin. As you pour the mangosteen with one hand, use the other hand to massage it into your scalp and hair so it does not drip off your head.

4. Repeat Step 3 with other sections of your scalp that need treatment. Apply a second or third coat if necessary.

5. When you have applied all the mangosteen, gently massage it into your scalp—unless doing so causes pain or irritation. Then brush or comb your hair. Let your hair air-dry or cover your head with a towel or an old shower-cap.

6. Leave the mangosteen in your hair for at least fifteen minutes and as long as overnight. Then rinse it out and wash your hair.

Optional: Wrap a towel around your neck and shoulders to protect your clothing from any mangosteen that may spill off your head.

MORE ABOUT THE MANGOSTEEN SCALP TREATMENT:

Repeat this procedure daily until the condition improves. You may need someone's help to pour the mangosteen, especially if you find it difficult to reach your arms up over your head. Daily treatment may fit more easily into your lifestyle if you do the treatment before you take a shower or before bedtime to wear overnight.

The rind particles can be difficult to wash completely out of your hair, especially if you have thick hair. This is why I suggest separating the particles as described in Step 2.

The Mangosteen Scalp Treatment may make your scalp feel tingly and warm. This sensation may be caused by extra blood moving to the treated area, and can be soothing for headaches and itchiness. But if it is uncomfortable, rinse your hair immediately. If you would still like to use mangosteen for a scalp condition, next time mix the mangosteen with an equal amount of water before applying it to your head.

If you have a problem in only a very small area of your scalp, try Smooth Mangosteen Paste (page 177) or a Mangosteen Mini-Poultice (page 169).

Section 2: Topical Applications

53.

Mangosteen Sitz Bath

A bath of mangosteen? Well, almost.

TRY THE MANGOSTEEN SITZ BATH FOR:

- Conditions of the anus.
- Conditions of the bladder and urethra.
- Conditions of the male genital organs.
- Conditions of the vagina and labia.
- Hemorrhoids.
- Hernias.
- Menstrual cramps.
- Vaginal yeast infections.

HOW TO TAKE A MANGOSTEEN SITZ BATH:

1. Fill the bathtub with three inches of hot water. Use water that is hotter than you would normally add to a bathtub as it will cool faster in the relatively shallow depth. Plus, the extra heat will enhance the ability of mangosteen's healing compounds to enter your body through your skin.

2. Hold a sealed bottle of mangosteen upside down and shake it gently until the pulp and rind particles are mixed throughout.

3. Pour three ounces of mangosteen into a measuring cup.

4. Take the measuring cup with you into the bathroom and pour the mangosteen into the bath water. Use the bathwater to rinse out all the rind particles from the bottom of the measuring cup.

5. Step into the water. Sit down slowly to give yourself time to acclimate to the hot water. When you are seated, keep your knees bent so that the only parts of your body in the water are your feet and bottom.

6. Rest in the tub for at least fifteen minutes or until the water cools. Every so often, move your hands through the water to keep the mangosteen pulp and rind well mixed throughout the bath water. The mangosteen water will be very soothing to your bottom.

MORE ABOUT THE MANGOSTEEN SITZ BATH:

If you think you might get chilly while sitting in a tub with relatively little water, wear an old t-shirt or wrap yourself with a towel that you don't mind getting wet.

You can also add other herbs or herbal teas to the bath water that are appropriate for your condition.

Adding three ounces of mangosteen to the bathwater is a suggested minimum amount. Feel free to add more if you feel your condition warrants it.

Bending your knees, as described in Step 5, is therapeutic for two reasons. First, it allows mangosteen's healing compounds to focus on your bottom. If your legs were submerged during the bath, these compounds would be diverted to them as well. Second, the feet have acupuncture points and meridians that connect to every organ and area of the body. The heated mangosteen-water will indirectly stimulate the entire body through these points.

When you are finished with the bath, you will not need to rinse yourself off before getting out. The mangosteen particles fall to the bathtub floor and do not stick to your body.

Section 2: Topical Applications

54.

Mangosteen Sunburn Treatment

Not only for sunburn, use this treatment for countless other topical applications. It also provides the soothing and healing effects of aloe vera.

TRY THE MANGOSTEEN SUNBURN TREATMENT FOR:

- Bites.
- Chaffing.
- Chapped lips.
- Cold sores.
- First aid.
- Itchy skin.
- Minor burns.
- Rashes.
- Skin irritations.
- Sunburn.
- And as a moisturizing lotion for sensitive skin.

HOW TO MAKE AND APPLY THE MANGOSTEEN SUNBURN TREATMENT:

1. Turn a bottle of mangosteen upside down and shake it gently to thoroughly mix the pulp and rind particles with the rest of the juice.

2. Pour about one ounce of the mangosteen into a medicine cup.

3. Wait about a minute for the heavier rind particles to sink to the bottom of the medicine cup.

4. Measure one-half teaspoonful of the rind-free mangosteen from the top of the medicine cup. Pour this into a second medicine cup or a small bowl.

5. Drink what is left of the ounce of mangosteen you originally poured. Count this as part of your total daily dosage of mangosteen.

6. Add one teaspoonful of aloe vera gel to the one-half teaspoonful of mangosteen. Use a cotton swab to mix the two ingredients. Stir until the mixture blends together completely.

7. Use the cotton swab to spread the mangosteen-aloe mixture over the area to be treated.

MORE ABOUT THE MANGOSTEEN SUNBURN TREATMENT:

This recipe omits the rind particles in mangosteen juice because they can irritate sensitive and sunburned skin when you try to wash them off, plus they would show on the skin.

If the area is relatively small, as with an insect bite or small rash, apply the mangosteen-aloe mixture very thickly and cover it with an adhesive strip or gauze pad. For large areas of the body, such as for sunburn, spread the mixture thinly and let it air dry. It will feel cold on the skin, which will be heavenly relief for sunburn sufferers. Make more batches of the Mangosteen Sunburn Treatment and reapply as needed. Aloe vera can be bought at health food stores and is available as a juice or gel. Either juice or gel can be used for the Mangosteen Sunburn Treatment. However the gel is thicker and allows you to apply a thicker coat of the mangosteen-aloe mixture, which means more healing compounds for your skin.

Section 2: Topical Applications of Mangosteen

Both aloe vera and mangosteen work synergistically when applied to the skin. Both have antibacterial, antiviral, analgesic, and anti-inflammatory, plus moisturizing and skin-conditioning properties.

If you would like to try a sunburn treatment using only mangosteen, see the Mangosteen Rash Plaster on page 183 or the Easy Mangosteen Skin Conditioner on page 195.

Section 2: Topical Applications

55. The Easy Mangosteen Skin Conditioner

An easy way to improve the health of your skin.

TRY THE EASY MANGOSTEEN SKIN CONDITIONER FOR:

- Daily skin-care maintenance on relatively small areas.
- Counteracting the effects of aging.
- Skin conditions of any kind.
- Skin problems anywhere on your body.

HOW TO APPLY THE EASY MANGOSTEEN SKIN CONDITIONER:

1. Gently shake a sealed bottle of mangosteen upside down until the rind particles are mixed throughout the juice.

2. Pour your regular daily dose of mangosteen into a medicine cup.

3. Wait a few seconds for the rind particles to begin to settle, and then pour a drop or two of particle-free mangosteen into the palm of your hand. Squeeze the medicine cup to control how much comes out.

4. Spread the drops of mangosteen over the skin that you want to treat until it soaks in.

5. Drink the remainder of your dose. Be sure to also consume the rind particles at the bottom of the medicine cup.

MORE ABOUT THE EASY
MANGOSTEEN SKIN CONDITIONER:

The Easy Mangosteen Skin Conditioner technique is worth mentioning because it is so very easy to do and its effects are so beneficial for the skin. It is also easy to incorporate this procedure into your daily routine and it only takes a few seconds.

Throughout this book I have referred to pouring doses of mangosteen into plastic medicine cups. For this treatment, they are essential. Pliable plastic medicine cups make it easy to pour just a few drops of liquid without spilling or over-pouring.

If you would like to keep a greater amount of mangosteen in contact with the skin for a longer period of time, try the Mangosteen Rash Plaster on page 183.

56.

Mangosteen Toe Treatment

Something else you can do with mangosteen's rind particles.

TRY THIS PROCEDURE FOR CONDITIONS SUCH AS:

- Athlete's foot.
- Foot fungus.
- Itchiness between the toes.
- Itchy toes.
- Toenail conditions.

HOW TO DO THE MANGOSTEEN TOE TREATMENT:

1. First, isolate some mangosteen rind particles as follows: Hold a sealed bottle of mangosteen upside down and shake it gently so that the mangosteen particles are well mixed throughout the juice. Immediately pour one ounce of mangosteen into a medicine cup. Let the medicine cup sit undisturbed for about five minutes. Carefully drink the juice portion of the mangosteen, which has risen to the top. This can count as one of your daily doses of mangosteen. Try to avoid drinking the particles. When you are finished, the particles should be resting on the bottom of the medicine cup, wet with a little juice.

2. Get a pair of socks and sit down with your socks and the medicine cup of mangosteen particles within reach. Scoop up some particles with a fingertip. Apply the particles between your toes, under your toenails or over the areas that need treatment. If all your toes are itchy, for example, try to put some mangosteen rind particles between each of them. The wet particles should be sticky enough to adhere to your skin. When all the particles have been applied, put on the socks.

3. Keep the socks on for a few hours or overnight, and then remove them. Most of the particles will have dried and fallen off your toes and are now inside the socks. Turn them inside-out and brush the leftover particles off into the trash. Or simply shake the socks outside. Then throw the socks into the wash. If your feet are sweaty, the particles may have stayed in place. In this case, remove your socks right before you step into the shower. This will avoid getting the particles on the floor.

MORE ABOUT THE MANGOSTEEN TOE TREATMENT:

If you typically wear socks during the day, it is easy to keep the mangosteen particles working for you all day long. If you don't, then you'll have to do this treatment at bedtime.

Apply this treatment daily until your symptoms improve.

If your toe condition is serious, collect mangosteen rind particles with each dose of mangosteen that you take. Keep them moist with a few drops of mangosteen juice, put them in an airtight container and store in the refrigerator until you are ready to apply them.

You may find that the itchiness may not go away on contact. But within a few hours you should notice that it is significantly relieved. This is because it can take some time for mangosteen's healing compounds to penetrate the skin and act upon the ailing cells.

SECTION 3
Internal Application of Mangosteen

Drinking mangosteen and applying it topically are the two most obvious uses of mangosteen. But this remarkable juice can also be therapeutic in ways that one might not expect. If it seems too odd to use mangosteen in some of the ways suggested in the following chapters, don't think of mangosteen as a juice drink. Think of it as the product of a medicinal fruit which contains special healing compounds.

This Section includes some procedures for using mangosteen in the mouth. They are not "drinking" applications per se, nor are they "topical," so I've included them here.

When you use mangosteen internally, plan to drink doses of mangosteen as well. To decide how much mangosteen to drink, select a procedure from Section 1 that best suits your condition. Drinking mangosteen will enhance the benefits of the internal application you are using. The reverse is also true, as internal applications draw the healing compounds from mangosteen that you drink to those parts of the body where the mangosteen is applied.

57.

The Auto-Distribution Dose

This procedure is based on the observation that the essence of a healing substance that is placed under the tongue will be distributed throughout the body within seconds.

TRY THIS PROCEDURE:

- To obtain the maximum benefit from a sip of mangosteen.
- To improve the effectiveness of your mangosteen doses.
- To feel more calm and centered emotionally or mentally.
- To reduce stress.
- To balance your body's energies.
- When simply drinking mangosteen doesn't give you the results you were hoping for.

HOW TO TAKE AN AUTO-DISTRIBUTION DOSE:

1. Hold a sealed bottle of mangosteen upside down and shake it gently until the pulp and rind particles are well mixed throughout the juice. Pour out a dose of about one teaspoonful. This should be enough to do this procedure two times.

2. Take a small sip of mangosteen (about one-half teaspoonful) and hold it underneath your tongue. Make sure the top of your tongue is up against the roof of your mouth. Put the front of

your tongue against the back of your lower front teeth. This is a natural position for your tongue and it will help to seal the mangosteen underneath your tongue.

3. Hold the mangosteen under your tongue for as long as possible. During this time, saliva will naturally mix with the mangosteen. Swallow as needed. Soon enough, an insignificant amount of mangosteen will remain under your tongue. Simply swallow what remains.

MORE ABOUT THE AUTO-DISTRIBUTION DOSE:

When a healing substance is held under the tongue, its essence, or healing energy, is somehow distributed throughout the body. Many people have actually felt this occur using a variety of healing substances. But the concept also holds true for mangosteen. When the essence of a healing substance like mangosteen is distributed throughout the body, the cells respond as if they had actually absorbed the healing compounds themselves. When these healing compounds do eventually arrive via the body's circulatory system, the cells are then able to absorb them more readily and make better use of them.

Receiving the healing energy of a substance also helps the cells relax. The stress of being undernourished, ill or laden with toxins seems to abate. This can lead to a feeling of centeredness on a whole-body level, and the causes of stress in our daily lives can feel less daunting.

Use this procedure as often as you like. You could incorporate it into all your doses by taking the first sip of each dose following the Auto-Distribution procedure. As this procedure increases the availability and absorption of mangosteen's healing compounds, you might then need to take less mangosteen in order to obtain the same results.

The Auto-Distribution Dose is the best way for someone debilitated with illness to take mangosteen. Use an eyedropper to place a few drops under the person's tongue.

58. The Mangosteen Enema

A relatively small amount of mangosteen in an enema bag is all you may need.

TRY A MANGOSTEEN ENEMA FOR CONDITIONS SUCH AS:

- Allergies.
- Bloating.
- Candidiasis.
- Constipation.
- Colitis.
- Crohn's disease.
- Detoxification.
- Diarrhea brought on by antibiotics.
- Diverticulitis.
- Heavy metal poisoning.
- Inflammation.
- Intestinal infections.
- Parasites.
- And as part of a semi-annual cleansing and re-nourishment program for the body.

HOW TO TAKE A MANGOSTEEN ENEMA:

1. Add warm water to a standard, two-quart enema bag until it is nearly full. If your tap water is chlorinated, use heated purified water. Test the temperature of the water in the bag with your finger to make sure it isn't too hot.

2. Hold a sealed bottle of mangosteen upside down and shake it until the rind particles are well mixed throughout the juice. Measure the amount of mangosteen you would like to add to the enema bag. Try one-half ounce to two ounces.

3. Add the mangosteen juice (including the rind particles) to the enema bag. Attach one end of the enema tube to the bag and the other end of the tube to the enema applicator. The tube should also be threaded through a squeezable flow-stopper. Lubricate the applicator with an herbal ointment. Don't use a mentholated ointment—it will sting!

4. Put the enema bag in the sink, hold the tube up, and press the bag to force any air trapped in the bag to exit through the tube. When mangosteen-water starts to come out of the bag, squeeze the flow-stopper. This will stop the flow of the liquid.

5. Hook the enema bag onto a shower door or the bathroom door handle or a towel rack. Place an old towel on the bathroom floor. Find a comfortable position on the floor. For instance, you could lie on one side, or lean over on your hands and knees.

6. Insert the applicator into your body. Release the stopper that is attached to the tube. Try to relax, in order to allow the liquid to enter your intestines. Squeeze the stopper as needed to regulate the flow of the mangosteen-water into your body.

7. When you feel an urge to expel the liquid, squeeze the stopper and remove the applicator from your body. Try to retain the liquid for a few minutes. Some people are able to retain the entire contents of the enema bag. Others can only retain a

portion of the enema at a time. If you were able to successfully retain the liquid, try massaging your lower abdomen. This will help break up accumulation in your intestines. Massage in the direction that food usually goes when passing through the intestines—looking down at your abdomen, this would be in a clockwise circle. Insert more mangosteen-water when you can.

8. When you are ready, expel the enema into the toilet.

MORE ABOUT THE MANGOSTEEN ENEMA:

A Mangosteen Enema brings mangosteen's anti-inflammatory properties directly to the intestines. This can often be more helpful for irritated intestines than drinking mangosteen simply because it takes so long for the mangosteen healing compounds to reach the intestines. Oral doses of mangosteen are still important however, to nourish, tone, and condition the intestines indirectly. Mangosteen's anti-inflammatory properties also soothe the intestines, thus reducing the stress of the enema itself.

Mangosteen also promotes the growth of a beneficial, probiotic, non-colonizing strain of yeast called Saccharomyces boulardii. S. boulardii has been found to produce lactic acid and some B vitamins, inactivate bacterial toxins, stimulate intestinal immune response, and protect against intestinal infections and harmful strains of yeast.* This makes mangosteen a particularly effective treatment for intestinal conditions.

Mangosteen rind particles can help scour material from the intestinal walls. However, the particles can also get stuck in the enema bag and tube. So be sure to thoroughly rinse the bag and tube when you are finished, and wash the applicator with soap and water.

If you take enemas relatively often, experiment with different amounts of mangosteen in the enema bag. This way you can find an amount that suits you best.

During a detoxification crisis, mangosteen enemas can help calm and stabilize the body by flushing the toxins that have built up in the intestines.

You may add mangosteen along with other natural substances that are sometimes included in enemas, such as sea-salt and liquid chlorophyll.

---

* http://www.wellohwell.com/saccharomycesboulardii.htm

HERE ARE GUIDELINES FOR
HOW OFTEN TO TAKE THE MANGOSTEEN ENEMA:

- For acute, temporary conditions such as bloating, flatulence, and constipation you may need only one enema.
- For chronic constipation, use a Mangosteen Enema daily for a few days. Then use the enema two or three times per week. Taper off the number of times per week that you take the enema as your condition improves.
- For intestinal conditions, disease and parasites, first take an enema with a teaspoonful of mangosteen added, to flush the bowels. Then take a second enema, with two ounces of mangosteen added, to introduce mangosteen as high up into the intestine as you can. Try to retain this mangosteen-water enema for as long as possible before expelling it. Do this a few times a week.
- For conditions such as heavy metal poisoning and detoxification take the enema once a day for a week, using one tablespoonful of mangosteen per enema. Then take the enema every other day. Gradually decrease the frequency of the enemas to once a week. If symptoms recur, repeat this schedule.

As with all the procedures in this book, adjust the suggestions given here to meet your personal needs.

Section 3: Internal Applications

59.

The Mangosteen Gargle

Mangosteen's analgesic effect can alleviate a sore throat and its antiseptic properties can fight infection.

**TRY THE MANGOSTEEN GARGLE
FOR THROAT CONDITIONS INCLUDING:**

- Dry throat.
- Sore throat.
- Strep throat.
- Swollen glands.
- Tonsillitis.
- The onset of flu-like symptoms.

HOW TO GARGLE WITH MANGOSTEEN:

1. Take a large sip of mangosteen.

2. Tip your head back and gargle as usual. Allow the juice to gradually drip down your throat.

3. Continue gargling for at least twenty seconds, until you have swallowed all the mangosteen.

MORE ABOUT
THE MANGOSTEEN GARGLE:

Mangosteen has a soothing effect on an inflamed, irritated throat. So gargle as often as necessary throughout the day. Cold mangosteen taken directly from the refrigerator has an analgesic effect of its own. But some people may prefer gargling with warm Mangosteen Tea (page 75). Try this when you drink Mangosteen Tea to boost your immune system.

You may gargle with some, or all, of your daily dose of mangosteen that you would normally drink. If you have a sore throat and other cold symptoms, however, consider drinking more mangosteen than usual. See the Procedure for Acute Conditions (page 33) and the Mangosteen Sick-Day Prevention Dose (page 59).

Section 3: Internal Applications

60.

The Mangosteen Mouthwash

The Mangosteen Mouthwash will leave your teeth and mouth feeling fresh.

TRY THE MANGOSTEEN MOUTHWASH FOR MOUTH CONDITIONS INCLUDING:

- Bad Breath.
- Cancer in the mouth.
- Dry mouth or "cotton mouth."
- Gingivitis.
- Heavy-metal poisoning from amalgam fillings.
- Inflammation in the mouth.
- Mouth infections.
- Sores on the tongue, gums or inside the cheeks.
- Toothache.
- Thrush.

HOW TO USE THE MANGOSTEEN MOUTHWASH:

1. Gently shake an upside down bottle of mangosteen until the mangosteen particles are well mixed throughout. Then measure a one-ounce dose and pour it into a medicine cup.

2. Wait about two minutes for the mangosteen particles to settle to the bottom of the medicine cup.

3. Take a sip of the mangosteen from the top of the medicine cup.

4. Swish the mangosteen around your teeth and gums and every corner of your mouth.

5. Continue for a full minute and then spit out the mangosteen. You will have enough mangosteen left over in the medicine cup to drink as one of your daily doses of mangosteen.

MORE ABOUT THE MANGOSTEEN MOUTHWASH:

I suggest using one of your daily one-ounce doses to do the Mangosteen Mouthwash because you will need to pour enough mangosteen for the rind particles to separate, so you can take a sip from the particle-free juice. If you do the mouthwash with a sip that contains particles, they will get stuck in your teeth and gums, which can be uncomfortable and annoying. You will need only a sip for this procedure so you won't be taking away from your daily dose.

For the first few seconds after taking the sip, the mangosteen may taste very tangy. But soon the tanginess abates and the mangosteen becomes sweeter. As time goes by, the taste will continue to change until it becomes somewhat taste free. If the taste becomes unpleasant, spit out the mangosteen. This may indicate that the mangosteen has absorbed toxins that are affecting the flavor. In this case, repeat the mouthwash procedure with another sip from the same dose.

For acute conditions, try the Mangosteen Mouthwash six to eight times a day. Simply leave an ounce of mangosteen in a medicine cup on the bathroom counter and do the procedure each time you visit the bathroom. For chronic conditions, try two or three daily applications. In this case, do the procedure with each dose of mangosteen that you take. If you are following the Procedure for Chronic Conditions (page 37), or a Health Improvement Procedure (page 39 and 41), you will naturally be taking at least three doses of mangosteen a day.

The Mangosteen Mouthwash can draw toxins from the surface of the mouth, whereas the Oral Detox (page 213) tends to draw them from deeper inside the tissue. Because the Mangosteen Mouthwash can draw toxins, avoid swallowing during the mouthwash procedure.

It is important to swish the mangosteen for the entire minute, or until the taste changes. This way, the enzymes in your saliva can break down the sugars so they will be less likely to cause tooth decay.

If you have a mouth condition that you can pinpoint, such as a sore or an area of infection try this:

1. Pour your daily one-ounce dose of mangosteen. Let the rind particles settle.

2. Do the Mangosteen Mouthwash Procedure.

3. Then drink almost all the watery portion of the juice, leaving about one-half teaspoonful behind—it will be rich with mangosteen pulp and particles.

4. Press a small piece of cotton ball into the mangosteen. It should soak up the remaining juice and be covered with the leftover mangosteen pulp and particles.

5. Use this as a Tooth and Gum Compress (page 221) by placing the pulpy side of the cotton against the affected area. Leave the cotton in place for five to fifteen minutes, or longer if possible.

65 Ways to Use Mangosteen

Section 3: Internal Applications

61.

The Oral Detox

When mangosteen is held in prolonged contact with the roof of the mouth, mangosteen's healing energies flood the head. This can be nourishing and healing and can encourage detoxification.

TRY THE ORAL DETOX FOR CONDITIONS IN THE:

- Brain.
- Ears.
- Eyes.
- Head.
- Mouth.
- Sinuses.
- Throat.

**CONDITIONS FOR WHICH YOU
COULD TRY THE ORAL DETOX INCLUDE:**

- Headache.
- Depression.
- Cancer.
- Earaches.
- Fever.
- Flu symptoms.
- Sinusitis.
- Common cold symptoms.
- Heavy-metal poisoning.
- Chemical toxicity.

HOW TO DO THE ORAL DETOX:

1. Gently shake a sealed bottle of mangosteen, while holding it upside down, to thoroughly mix the pulp and rind particles with the rest of the juice.

2. Measure one tablespoonful of mangosteen and pour it into a medicine cup or teacup.

3. Take a sip and trap the mangosteen on top of your tongue and against the roof of your mouth. Secure it there by gently pressing the edges of your tongue against the inside of your upper teeth. This will also discourage saliva from mixing with the mangosteen. Hold the sip in your mouth for at least a minute or longer. Avoid swallowing the mangosteen but don't worry if some drips down your throat.

4. Then, spit out the mangosteen.

5. Rinse your mouth with purified water.

6. Repeat until the dose is used up. You should have enough for about three to five sips.

MORE ABOUT THE ORAL DETOX:

Start by doing the Oral Detox once a day for about a week. Then try it twice a day if you are feeling well, it is helping you and think you can handle a stronger detoxification. If necessary, and if it is helpful, do the Oral Detox several times a day until symptoms abate. Depending on your condition, this may take from a few days to many months. Make it part of your daily routine. For example, do the Oral Detox Procedure with the first one or two sips of your regular daily doses and then drink the rest.

During this procedure, mangosteen will start to mobilize toxins out of cells throughout the head but will start with those nearest the roof of the mouth.

If you are doing this procedure for mercury or heavy-metal poisoning, undiluted mangosteen may have too strong an effect and may cause an uncomfortable cleansing reaction. To avoid this, mix a teaspoonful of mangosteen in half a glass of water and use a sip of this to do the Oral Detox.

Do not underestimate the cleansing potential of the Oral Detox. If detoxification happens too quickly, you may get a headache or experience other cleansing symptoms (page 233). Drink plenty of purified water to help flush the toxins from your body. Indeed, even though it is suggested that you hold the mangosteen against the roof of your mouth for a minute, spit out the mangosteen sooner if you feel light-headed or have any other discomfort. If the Oral Detox causes too strong a cleansing reaction, do the Oral Detox less frequently. Or mix the mangosteen with some water before you use it for the Oral Detox.

The Oral Detox may ease head and mouth pain. It may also contribute to increased mental clarity and improved memory. Other side benefits can include relief from conditions such as gingivitis, infections, toothache and mouth sores.

65 Ways to Use Mangosteen

Section 3: Internal Applications

62.

The Mangosteen Rectal Implant

Not a place you might expect to put a fruit juice! But if you have problems in this area, you may be glad you did.

TRY THE MANGOSTEEN RECTAL IMPLANT FOR:

- Cancer of the bowel, colon or rectum.
- Diverticulitis.
- Fissures.
- Hemorrhoids.
- Inflammation.
- And other bowel and rectal conditions.

HOW TO DO THE MANGOSTEEN RECTAL IMPLANT:

1. Purchase a four-ounce disposable enema bottle from the drugstore. Use it as directed and then clean it thoroughly. Or, open the bottle and pour the pre-packaged liquid down the drain.

2. Shake a sealed bottle of mangosteen upside down until the rind particles are well mixed with the rest of the juice.

3. Pour the amount of mangosteen that you want to use into a measuring cup that has a lip for pouring. (Most one-cup measuring cups do.) Try one or two ounces of mangosteen. If

you want to use less than that, say one tablespoonful, then add about an equal amount of water to make insertion easier.

4. Pour the mangosteen into the enema bottle. Remove the circular rubber valve from inside the applicator tube so the rind particles won't clog it up. Affix the applicator tube to the enema bottle. The tube is usually prepared with lubricating ointment, but if you think you need more apply it now.

5. Find a comfortable position on the floor, either lying on one side, lying on your back, bending over the sink or leaning over on your hands and knees. Put a towel beneath you in case of spills. Better yet, avoid the extra laundry by doing the implant in an empty bathtub.

6. Insert the applicator into your rectum. Hold the bottle upside down, and then squeeze the bottle to release the mangosteen into your body. Since you have removed the valve from the applicator, be sure to remove the enema from your body before your release your grip on the bottle.

7. Hold the mangosteen in your body for as long as possible. Try to keep it in for at least five minutes. In most cases, one or two ounces of liquid inserted into the rectum is easily retained.

8. When you are finished, rinse out the bottle and wash the applicator tip very well with water and antiseptic soap if you want to reuse the same bottle and applicator.

MORE ABOUT THE MANGOSTEEN RECTAL IMPLANT:

If you have a condition of the lower bowel or rectum, it is especially important to apply mangosteen there directly. When you drink mangosteen, its healing compounds spread throughout your body. But not enough of them are likely to reach the lower bowel and rectum to be adequately therapeutic—though they will help your condition indirectly by uplifting your overall health.

Section 3: Internal Applications

For this procedure it is unnecessary to separate out the rind particles. In fact they may even act as roughage to help scour accumulation from the intestinal walls. Mangosteen rind also has healing compounds that are particularly helpful to the intestines, as traditional remedies include the rind specifically for that purpose (see pages 80-81).

Ideally, try to do the Rectal Implant after you have had a bowel movement. Then your rectum will be empty and mangosteen's healing compounds will be more accessible to the ailing tissue. In fact, if your rectum is full, you may have to squeeze the enema bottle quite hard to empty it into your body. If you take an enema beforehand to clear your bowels, expel as much of the enema into the toilet as possible before doing the Rectal Implant. If too much water remains in your body, you may have a harder time retaining the implant.

If you do have an urge to expel the implant, try to keep the implant in your body for at least a few minutes, and then follow the urge. This urge may be your body's way of flushing toxins that the mangosteen has helped release. If your body has an immediate strong urge to expel the implant, use less mangosteen next time.

If the rectum is highly irritated, the mangosteen might burn slightly at first. Soothing relief should soon follow. But next time, mix the mangosteen with an equal amount of water before inserting it into your body.

Perform the implant daily if your condition is relatively serious. When symptoms subside, gradually reduce the number of times you do the implant per week. Remember to support your Internal Mangosteen Application with a Mangosteen Drinking Procedure (see Section 1) that is appropriate for your condition.

65 Ways to Use Mangosteen

Section 3: Internal Applications

63.

The Tooth and Gum Compress

The gums are particularly receptive to mangosteen's anti-inflammatory and antiseptic healing compounds.

USE THE MANGOSTEEN TOOTH AND GUM COMPRESS FOR:

- Gum infection.
- Helping to heal an area after dental work.
- Isolated areas of thrush.
- Mercury spots.
- Mouth sores.
- Tooth infection and toothache.

HOW TO MAKE AND APPLY THE TOOTH AND GUM COMPRESS:

1. Prepare a compress pad using either a cotton ball or sterile gauze. If you use cotton, form it into a cylinder about two inches long and about one-quarter inch wide. If you use gauze, roll it into a cylinder of about the same size.

2. Turn a sealed bottle of mangosteen upside down and shake it gently until the pulp and rind particles are mixed throughout the juice.

3. Pour a teaspoonful of mangosteen into a small bowl.

4. Press the compress pad into the mangosteen. Wipe up any pulp and rind particles that remain in the bowl with the pulpy side of the compress pad.

5. Insert the wet compress pad into your mouth over the affected area. The pulpy side of the pad should be against your skin. It is okay to swallow the mangosteen that will naturally leak out. But swallowing also tends to draw more mangosteen out of the compress.

6. Leave the compress pad in place for ten to fifteen minutes. By then, much of the mangosteen in the compress pad will have been swallowed and replaced with saliva. Even so, the pulp and rind that cling to the compress pad will still be therapeutic.

7. Remove the compress pad and discard it. Repeat this procedure as often as needed.

MORE ABOUT THE MANGOSTEEN TOOTH AND GUM COMPRESS:

Even if the condition occupies a small area, make the compress pad as big as suggested and treat the entire portion of the jaw where the condition is located. By using a relatively large compress pad, more of mangosteen's healing compounds will be available to the area.

People have different levels of pain tolerance and sensitivity, so the analgesic effects of this treatment will vary.

Apply the Mangosteen Tooth and Gum Compress both before dental work to reduce any traumatic effects you may experience. Also apply it afterwards to promote healing. Also, try taking a Trauma Dose as soon as possible before dental work begins, to help you relax and better handle the stress involved.

For gum infections and abscesses, see also The Mangosteen Tooth and Gum Pack on page 223.

Section 3: Internal Applications

64.

The Tooth and Gum Pack

Here is another way to use mangosteen rind particles.

**THIS TREATMENT
CAN BE HELPFUL FOR:**

- Abscesses.
- Gum infections.
- Gum inflammation.
- Tooth pain.

**HOW TO DO THE MANGOSTEEN
TOOTH AND GUM PACK:**

1. If you don't already have some leftover mangosteen rind particles, prepare some as follows:

    a. Hold a sealed bottle of mangosteen upside down and shake it gently so that the mangosteen particles are well mixed throughout the juice.
    b. Immediately pour one ounce of mangosteen into a medicine cup. Let the medicine cup sit undisturbed for about five minutes.
    c. Carefully drink the juice portion of the mangosteen, which has risen to the top of the medicine cup. This can count as one of your daily doses of mangosteen. Try to avoid drinking the particles. When you are finished, the particles will be wet with pulp and a little juice.

2. Scoop up the particles with your fingertip. Carefully place the particles inside your mouth and on the area you want to treat. Press the particles between the affected gums and the teeth, and also between the teeth. Continue until you have placed all the mangosteen particles.

3. Keep the particles in place for as long as possible. At first, their presence may cause you to salivate, but this should soon abate as your mouth grows accustomed to the particles being there.

Optional: Using your fingertips to apply the rind particles, as described in Step 2, takes a minimum of effort. However, you could instead use a piece of a cotton ball to wipe up the leftover rind and pulp from step 1. Then press the pulpy side of the cotton against the affected area.

MORE ABOUT THE MANGOSTEEN TOOTH AND GUM PACK:

This procedure is best done at bedtime, when you can rest and the mangosteen particle pack has a better chance of staying in place. If a painful condition demands that you try this treatment during the day, avoid talking as this will displace the particles sooner.

The Mangosteen Mouthwash (page 209) can also be helpful. Try it before you do the Tooth and Gum Pack, or during the day when doing the Pack is inconvenient.

Section 3: Internal Applications

65.

Mangosteen Vaginal Wipe

A fast and easy way to alleviate minor discomforts.

WHEN TO USE THE MANGOSTEEN VAGINAL WIPE:

- For conditions located on the labia or just inside the vagina.
- Vaginal itching.
- Yeast infections.
- To soothe chapped, irritated or dry labia.

HOW TO APPLY THE MANGOSTEEN VAGINAL WIPE:

1. Shake a sealed bottle of mangosteen, held upside down, until the rind particles are thoroughly mixed with the rest of the juice.

2. Pour one tablespoonful into a medicine cup.

3. Measure one tablespoonful of purified water and add this to the medicine cup. Let the rind particles settle.

4. Pour the top portion of the mangosteen-water into a second medicine cup, leaving the rind particles behind.

5. Take the particle-free mangosteen-water with you to the bathroom. Dip half a sterile cotton ball into the liquid. Only one side of the cotton needs to be wet.

6. Wipe the wet side of the cotton ball inside the vaginal opening and between the labia. Squeeze the cotton ball as you apply it, or press it against your body to release the mangosteen onto your skin. Hold the cotton against particularly sore or itchy areas.

7. Drop the used cotton ball into the toilet. Pat yourself dry with some toilet paper. Use a panty-liner to protect your clothing from any remaining mangosteen that might otherwise stain.

MORE ABOUT THE MANGOSTEEN VAGINAL WIPE:

This procedure can be done after every urination or as needed. Simply keep the medicine cup on the bathroom counter. The mangosteen will stay fresh for a couple days, and you should have enough for many applications.

Mangosteen's anti-fungal, antiseptic and anti-inflammatory healing compounds can make this technique very effective for relatively minor complaints. Relief may come on contact or a few minutes later. For more serious conditions, you will need to use more mangosteen and keep it in place longer. Try the Mangosteen Poultice (page 179). You could also increase the effectiveness of the Mangosteen Vaginal Wipe by inserting the mangosteen-soaked cotton ball between your labia and keeping it there for a few hours. Replace it several times a day with another cotton ball soaked in mangosteen.

I suggest mixing mangosteen with water for this application to reduce the possibility that the mangosteen might burn particularly chaffed, raw or sensitive skin. If the application is still uncomfortable, wait a few minutes to see if the feeling subsides. If it does not improve, rinse the area with a cotton ball soaked in water.

Be careful not to get any rind particles inside your vagina, as they have no natural means for getting out and could cause irritation.

APPENDIX 1
Health Evaluation Questionnaire

Healing is a natural function of our body. It is also natural to forget we ever had certain symptoms once they have gone away. This Health Evaluation Questionnaire will help you remember the symptoms you once had so you can better appreciate your health improvements. Use this questionnaire as your personal testimony to the effects of mangosteen.

You are welcome to make copies of the questionnaire for personal use in evaluating the effects of mangosteen. To get the most benefit from this questionnaire, do not look back at copies you have previously completed until you are finished filling out a new copy. Then you can be more objective about the changes in your health. Keep this information confidential or share it with your doctor, family, friends and associates.

USE THE HEALTH EVALUATION QUESTIONNAIRE TO:

- Keep track of your health progress.
- Evaluate how well mangosteen is helping you.
- Evaluate the effectiveness of certain mangosteen dosages and applications.
- Calculate your Health Index.

YOUR HEALTH INDEX:

Your Health Index is a numerical value that rates your current state of health. It is very easy to calculate and can help you objectively evaluate how well mangosteen has been working for you. The lower your Health Index number, the healthier you probably are. The higher the number, the more support your body needs in order to heal. You can find your Health Index by completing the Health Evaluation Questionnaire and follow the directions on page 231.

Before you take mangosteen for the first time, complete the Questionnaire and find your Health Index. Then try mangosteen for a month and again complete the Health Evaluation Questionnaire and figure out your Health Index. As your health improves your index will get lower. According to the way the questionnaire was constructed, the lowest possible index number is 30, and the highest is 150. Because the range of possible Health Index numbers is relatively narrow, even a drop of only a few points is significant.

Monitor your health improvement by filling out a copy of the Health Evaluation Questionnaire once a month and then finding your Health Index for that month. A chart on page 232 will help you keep track of your results.

Compare your Health Index with the mangosteen procedures you have been following that month. Experiment with different procedures to see how much your Health Index can improve!

Appendix 1: Health Evaluation Questionnaire

THE HEALTH EVALUATION QUESTIONNAIRE

Name:_____

Date: _____ Body Weight:_____

The primary condition/symptoms for which I am taking mangosteen:

_____

Rate the following on a scale from 1 to 5 and circle your answer.

1 = No symptoms.
2 = Occasional symptoms or mild symptoms.
3 = Frequent symptoms or moderate symptoms.
4 = Daily symptoms that are tolerable.
5 = Daily symptoms that are bad or very painful.

1. My eyesight: **1 2 3 4 5**
2. My hearing: **1 2 3 4 5**
3. My mouth, gums and teeth: **1 2 3 4 5**
4. My throat and neck: **1 2 3 4 5**
5. My back and shoulders: **1 2 3 4 5**
6. My arms and legs, including elbows and knees: **1 2 3 4 5**
7. My hands and feet, including wrists and ankles: **1 2 3 4 5**
8. My circulation: **1 2 3 4 5**
9. My heart and cardiovascular health: **1 2 3 4 5**
10. My digestive tract, including stomach and colon: **1 2 3 4 5**
11. My blood sugar level: **1 2 3 4 5**
12. How I feel after I eat: **1 2 3 4 5**
13. My bowel regularity: **1 2 3 4 5**
14. My bladder and urinary tract: **1 2 3 4 5**
15. My lungs and bronchial tubes: **1 2 3 4 5**
16. Any allergies: **1 2 3 4 5**
17. My skin: **1 2 3 4 5**
18. How I feel when I wake up in the morning: **1 2 3 4 5**
19. How I feel when I go to bed at night: **1 2 3 4 5**

Appendix 1: Health Evaluation Questionnaire

20. How often I have pain anywhere in my body: **1 2 3 4 5**
21. How often I get headaches: **1 2 3 4 5**
22. My reproductive organs: **1 2 3 4 5**
23. My libido: **1 2 3 4 5**
24. My menstrual cycles (women): **1 2 3 4 5**
    My prostate (men): **1 2 3 4 5**
25. My emotional balance and self-control: **1 2 3 4 5**
26. My memory and mental clarity: **1 2 3 4 5**
27. Any feelings of depression: **1 2 3 4 5**
28. My energy level: **1 2 3 4 5**
29. My stamina (my endurance or ability to withstand illness, fatigue or hardship) : **1 2 3 4 5**
30. My immune system: **1 2 3 4 5**

Optional: List three symptoms, unique to your particular condition, that you would like to keep track of. If you plan to compare your Health Index number with that of your friends and family, do not include these three optional numbers when calculating your Health Index. Then, everyone's Health Index will be based on the same thirty questions above.

1. _____: **1 2 3 4 5**
2. _____: **1 2 3 4 5**
3. _____: **1 2 3 4 5**

Note: You are welcome to make copies of this Health Evaluation Questionnaire only for personal use to evaluate the effects of mangosteen on your health.

CALCULATING YOUR HEALTH INDEX:

Add up the numbers you have circled above. Their sum is your Health Index.

My Health Index number is: _____

YOUR HEALTH INDEX
SUMMARY SHEET:

Observe the changes in your health by adding to this chart each time you complete a copy of the Health Evaluation Questionnaire.

Date Questionnaire Completed	My Health Index Number	Average Daily Dosage of Mangosteen I've taken this month
_____	_____	_____
_____	_____	_____
_____	_____	_____
_____	_____	_____
_____	_____	_____
_____	_____	_____
_____	_____	_____
_____	_____	_____
_____	_____	_____
_____	_____	_____
_____	_____	_____
_____	_____	_____

APPENDIX 2
Cleansing Reactions

Toxins are a part of life. They exist in our air, water and food and are also produced by the body as a result of its normal functioning. The body naturally cleanses itself of toxins and metabolic wastes in many ways. But often a backlog occurs. Toxins are stored and eventually they may contribute to disease. A healthy lifestyle supports the release of stored toxins. But sometimes, a healthful practice or supplement (like mangosteen), can cause your body to release more toxins than your organs can handle at once. The symptoms that result are called a "cleansing reaction," "healing crises" or "detoxification crises."

Obviously, it is best to avoid these symptoms with a slow but steady transition to a healthier lifestyle, which leads to gradual detoxification. But sometimes that is not possible, despite our best intentions. On the other hand, cleansing reactions don't happen to everyone and not all cleansing reactions are uncomfortable. Sometimes when our body releases toxins we enjoy renewed heath right away. This often results in what I call "positive cleansing reactions" (see page 239).

The following list of symptoms may indicate disease or infection, but if they occur soon enough after adding a healthful procedure or supplement to your lifestyle, they are likely cleansing reactions. This Appendix will help you identify cleansing reactions and give you some ideas about how to handle them.

COMMON CLEANSING REACTIONS CAN INCLUDE:

- Bad breath or body odor.
- Boils.
- Cough.
- Diarrhea or loose stools.
- Emotional releases.
- Fatigue.

- Foul smelling urine.
- Headaches.
- Heavier than usual bleeding at menstruation.
- Intestinal gas or bloating.
- Joint pain (sudden onset, not due to injury).
- Mucus discharge.
- Pimples.
- Skin rashes.
- Swollen glands.

HOW DO I KNOW IF I'M HAVING A CLEANSING REACTION?

Obviously, the symptoms listed above may also indicate disease or illness. To be considered a cleansing reaction, these symptoms need to have an obvious correlation to taking a healthful supplement, in this case, mangosteen. Indeed, it can sometimes be difficult to know if symptoms are actually due to a cleansing reaction and not the result of illness, allergy, hypersensitivity to mangosteen, dehydration or a true cleansing reaction. The following paragraphs discuss each of these options. Regardless, be sure to get medical attention if necessary.

If you get a reaction after taking mangosteen:

1. You may have an allergy to mangosteen.

    Suspect that this is the case if your symptoms begin after taking mangosteen the first time only and include your body's typical responses to things that you are allergic to. To find out if your reaction is an allergy, stop taking mangosteen, use the remedies that you usually take to control your allergies and wait until your symptoms subside. Then apply a small amount of mangosteen on your skin (page 195). If this gives you a rash or you get another sign of an allergy, you probably are allergic to mangosteen. It would be best not to take mangosteen at this time. If you have no symptoms with topical applications and if your first dose was one tablespoonful or more, reintroduce mangosteen into your diet starting with very small amounts. See Gradually Introducing Mangosteen to Your Diet on page 11.

Appendix 2: Cleansing Reactions

2. You might be hypersensitive to mangosteen's healing compounds. (In other words, taking too much stresses your body because a teaspoonful will do for you what one ounce might do for most other people.)

   Suspect that this is the case if your symptoms do not include your body's typical allergic responses, and if they begin after your first dose of mangosteen or after taking only a few doses. Your intuition might also let you know that you've taken too much and to reduce your doses next time. Another way to find out if you are hypersensitive to mangosteen is to stop taking mangosteen and wait until your symptoms subside. Then apply a small amount of mangosteen on your skin (page 195) to rule out allergy. If you do not get a rash or any other allergic reaction, try other topical applications. Give your body time to become accustomed to mangosteen. Then try Gradually Introducing Mangosteen to Your Diet (page 11).

3. You are dehydrated.

   Suspect this is the case if you have been drinking less than two or three glasses of water a day. As a result, it is very likely that toxins have been building up in your system. Most people need at least eight glasses of water a day to flush metabolic wastes as well as the toxins that the body collects from diet and the environment. If you are dehydrated and you get symptoms that you suspect might be a cleansing reaction, simply drink more water. If your symptoms are caused by dehydration, they can go away rather quickly. If this occurs, continue to drink this extra water and continue to take mangosteen to assist your body through the cleansing.

4. You may be having a cleansing reaction.

   Suspect that this is the case if you have been taking mangosteen for awhile without symptoms. Typical cleansing reactions often include foul odors, and they may or may not resemble your body's typical allergic responses. Cleansing reactions seem to have no explainable cause other than the healthful practice or supplement you have added to your lifestyle, or whose frequency or dosage you have recently increased. In hindsight, you can confirm a true cleansing reaction if, after the symptoms go away, you feel better than you did beforehand. After a cleansing reaction is over, you might also enjoy some degree of positive cleansing symptoms (page 239).

If you have been taking mangosteen for awhile and then get cleansing symptoms:
- You are probably not allergic to mangosteen or hypersensitive to its healing compounds, since you have been taking mangosteen for awhile without having a reaction.
- You may be experiencing the flu or the first symptoms of illness. See your doctor, especially if the symptoms do not go away after taking extra water (to eliminate a reaction due to dehydration) or after a few days.
- You may indeed be having a cleansing reaction.

It can be hard to know your symptoms are a cleansing reaction or the flu because:
- Both cleansing reactions and the flu tend to last the same amount of time. Both can be acute and short-lived, however both can also drag out for awhile.
- Natural methods for enhancing the immune system will help in either case.
- Antibiotics, cough suppressants and other pharmaceutical medicines can clear flu symptoms and suppress a cleansing reaction. Either way, they reduce symptoms and stabilize the body. Then the body can regain its strength for a more gradual detoxification later.

You probably have a cold or flu if:
You have been taking a Maintenance Dose of only one ounce daily. Generally, one ounce a day of mangosteen is enough to supply the body's daily requirement for mangosteen's healing compounds. It is unlikely that this much mangosteen would initiate a cleansing reaction in most people.

Appendix 2: Cleansing Reactions

You are especially likely to have a cleansing reaction if you are doing or have recently done:
- A Mangosteen Fast (pages 85, 89).
- The Technique for Stubborn Conditions (page 45).
- The Top Dose Procedure (page 49).
- Procedures that suggest taking three or more ounces of mangosteen per day.
- Or you have recently increased your daily dosage of mangosteen.

> **PLEASE USE COMMON SENSE WHEN TAKING MANGOSTEEN**
>
> See a health professional if your symptoms become uncomfortable or do not abate.

WHAT TO DO IF YOU THINK YOU ARE HAVING A CLEANSING REACTION:

Cleansing reactions are ultimately helpful to the body, albeit they can be uncomfortable. Do what you can to clear your body of the toxins it is trying to release. For example:

- Give yourself extra time to rest and sleep.
- Make sure you drink at least eight glasses of purified water a day. Water is essential to help flush toxins from the system.
- Try taking the same number of daily doses as usual but take only half the amount of mangosteen in each dose. Taking less mangosteen during a cleansing reaction can slow the release of toxins.
- On the other hand, adding more mangosteen to your diet than you usually drink can be helpful if you believe your cleansing reaction was initiated by something other than mangosteen. Try the Mangosteen Fast Method 2 (page 89).
- Try a Mangosteen Enema (page 203).
- Drink one of your daily mangosteen doses in the form of Mangosteen Tea (page 75). The hot liquid can be soothing and comforting, especially if you drink it when following the Mangosteen Anti-Stress Procedure (page 53).
- Take your doses of mangosteen (or at least one sip of every dose) following the Auto-Distribution Procedure (page 201).
- Combine mangosteen with other modalities to ease your symptoms. Mangosteen is compatible with all natural healing methods including: herbs, chiropractic, Chinese medicine, Ayurvedic medicine, vitamins and minerals, chelation therapy, acupuncture, massage and so forth.

In general, any reaction to mangosteen is better than no reaction at all. The cleansing reaction proves that your body recognizes mangosteen and that mangosteen can indeed help you. After the cleansing reaction is over, reevaluate the procedure for drinking mangosteen that you have been using. Consider focusing more on topical applications and reducing your daily dosage to allow your body to detoxify more gradually.

POSITIVE CLEANSING REACTIONS:

Although cleansing reactions have a reputation for being associated with unpleasant symptoms, they can also produce positive symptoms such as those below. Unfortunately, positive cleansing reactions do not last as long as we would like them to. Positive cleansing reactions almost always occur within the first few days or weeks after you add a health-supporting supplement like mangosteen to your diet, or after Interrupting Mangosteen Therapy (page 67), or even after you've had a true cleansing reaction.

Positive Reactions Include:
- Significantly improved memory.
- Remarkably clearer thinking.
- A surge of creativity.
- A greater sense of well-being.
- More energy than usual.
- Increased libido.
- More clarity, insights and new ideas.
- Dreams that are markedly more meaningful and easier to remember.
- A sudden ability to see the overview of life or the underlying purpose of various situations that we may be involved in.
- Unusual sensitivity to one's own thoughts, needs and feelings as well as those of others.
- A great deal of excitement and enthusiasm for mangosteen.

Positive cleansing reactions can be pronounced and obvious. Or they can be mild and perhaps unnoticeable—until they go away and then we miss them. Naturally, we welcome the positive reactions but try not to be disappointed when they ease. As your body adjusts to a new, healthier state of "normal," the positive reactions will lessen. Continue to take mangosteen to help maintain this higher level of health.

APPENDIX 3
What If Mangosteen Doesn't Seem To Work for Me?

If mangosteen does not seem to be helping you or is not working as fast as you would like, ask yourself the following questions. The answers may help you understand what may be happening and give you some ideas about what to do.

For what condition are you taking mangosteen?
It helps to decide why you are taking mangosteen. This makes it easier to correlate mangosteen's effects with changes in your health.

How long have you had this condition?
If your condition is chronic and longstanding, you may need more time on any health improvement program before you see results. In the process of healing, healthier cells replace sick or damaged cells. This always seems to take longer than one would like. You probably won't feel a difference in your health until enough of these replacements have been made.

How long have you been taking mangosteen?
In some cases, it can take several months before some people enjoy significant changes in their health, especially for chronic and serious conditions. Give mangosteen a fair chance to work and give yourself a fair opportunity to heal.

How much mangosteen are you taking?

Some people's bodies need more mangosteen than others do even for maintenance. In general, the more serious the condition, the more mangosteen you probably need.

Are you taking mangosteen regularly?

When addressing any health condition with mangosteen, take your doses regularly. Make sure you have enough mangosteen on hand so that you don't run out.

Have you filled out the Health Evaluation Questionnaire?

If it has been more than four weeks since you last filled out a copy, now is the time to fill out another copy. Take an honest look at how you used to feel and how you feel now. Is there any difference at all? Also ask a friend or family member to recall your state of health and well-being before you began taking mangosteen and then to evaluate your present state of health. This feedback will be invaluable. In fact, because it is objective, it can be more helpful than your own evaluation and may more accurately reveal how well mangosteen is actually working for you. In addition, find out if your Health Index has changed. The Health Index is another objective way to evaluate health improvement.

Have you noticed any improvements in minor discomforts?

It is easy to overlook these kinds of improvements, especially if you are taking mangosteen for a major health challenge.

Have you had any cleansing reaction symptoms since you started taking mangosteen?

For a list of common cleansing reactions, see page 233. Cleansing reactions, though generally uncomfortable, should be considered beneficial because they signal that the body is experiencing a major readjustment towards better health. Detoxification is often a necessary first step before cell repair and health building can begin.

Did mangosteen ever work for you at all?

There is a difference between the experience of not ever having noticed any effects from mangosteen at all, and the experience of noticing a difference at first and then nothing thereafter.

If you have never, ever noticed anything from mangosteen, and you have been taking mangosteen for a few months, then perhaps your body simply does not need mangosteen's healing compounds at this time.

If you noticed a difference at first, and then nothing since, you know that mangosteen can help you. But now it may be working below the threshold of your ability to perceive its effects. Or, it may be helping you to maintain your present level of health and preventing it from getting worse. If you suspect that this is the case, try increasing your daily dose of mangosteen. You might also try the Technique for Stubborn Conditions (page 45) or one of the Mangosteen Fasts (page 85, 89) or the Top Dose Procedure (page 49).

What about positive changes in your personality, emotions, mental clarity and memory?

Sometimes mangosteen seems to work on our non-physical aspects first. We may become more patient, calm, joyful, better able to handle stress and emotions, or feel less depressed, irritable, impatient or moody. Don't overlook these possible health benefits as well.

Are you taking other health supplements?

Mangosteen is not a cure-all. Although mangosteen provides a variety of important healing compounds and can address a long list of health concerns, it is possible that your condition would benefit from other healthful practices and supplements as well.

What activities do you now enjoy since you began to take mangosteen?

Sometimes the best measure of improved health is not our symptoms, but how well we can enjoy life.

65 Ways to Use Mangosteen

APPENDIX 4
What If My Symptoms Return?

Some people find that after mangosteen alleviates certain symptoms, these symptoms eventually return. It is tempting to say that mangosteen has stopped working. But this is not necessarily the case. Here are a few possible explanations, plus some ideas for how you can use mangosteen if your symptoms do come back.

- People who feel better almost immediately after starting mangosteen may be experiencing positive cleansing reactions (page 239), which may be making them feel so good they don't notice their symptoms. Unfortunately their symptoms will probably "return" when the positive cleansing reactions ease. Lasting positive changes in one's health will not occur until they are supported by actual changes in the cells. These changes usually take time.

- After taking mangosteen, many people find they can eat foods that once before caused symptoms such as indigestion, headaches or joint pain. They find they can work harder, play harder, go to bed later and get up earlier, too. Instead of using mangosteen's healing compounds to grow healthier, we often use them to help us get away with doing things that are stressful (albeit enjoyable). There is nothing wrong with this. But if we abuse the freedom, it won't last. When the body can no longer handle the added stress, we will again need more sleep, and favorite foods will again cause discomfort. Symptoms may appear to return when really they were not given the opportunity to heal properly in the first place.

- The body will continue to age and manifest stress at its weakest points—no matter how wonderful the therapies that we give to it. If new stresses are introduced into our lives, these weakest points may again reveal themselves and conditions that were once alleviated may return.

- During the healing process, pain and other symptoms may go away. But this does not mean our ailment is cured. It can take awhile for healthy cells to replace unhealthy cells. If we stop taking proper care of ourselves, we can cause additional stress on the healing tissue, and symptoms may return.

- Health improves in cycles: A period of health-building follows every period of well-being. This health-building period may pass unnoticed or make us feel more tired than usual. Or, it may include an intense cleansing when the body releases toxins, wastes, fat and various excesses that it may have been storing. As these toxins enter the bloodstream, they pass by our weak or problem areas. These toxins can irritate these areas, causing symptoms to temporarily resurface or get worse.

- Symptoms can be signals to take better care of ourselves. Recurring symptoms may be our body's best way to tell us we need something that we have not yet given to our body. For example, perhaps we need more rest or a nutrient that is missing or inadequate in our diet.

- Recurring symptoms may also alert us to look at our condition from another angle. Perhaps there are mental or emotional causes that we have been overlooking. Sometimes physical improvement cannot continue until we take care of the mental and emotional aspects of ourselves.

IF YOUR SYMPTOMS RETURN, HERE ARE SOME TECHNIQUES YOU COULD TRY:

- Try Interrupting Mangosteen Therapy (page 67).
- Read the chapter "The Mangosteen Maintenance Dose #3" (page 29) and incorporate the principles described in that chapter into whatever mangosteen drinking procedure you may be following.
- Take sips of your doses on a regular time schedule. For example, take a sip every five, fifteen or twenty minutes. Set a timer to ensure you keep to the rhythm. See the Mangosteen Detoxification Program (page 93).
- Follow the Auto-Distribution Procedure (page 201) with at least one sip from every mangosteen dose that you take.
- Try Sipping (page 19) your doses of mangosteen if you usually drink them All at Once (page 21). Or, vice versa.
- Follow the Technique for Stubborn Conditions (page 45).
- Examine your diet and your lifestyle. Are you taking part in any activities that might be stressing your body? Learn how to reduce and control stress. Find out what foods you may be allergic to and eliminate them from your diet. Some health practitioners have ways to test for allergies that can give you immediate feedback. Get more rest, try meditation or spiritual exercise and take better care of yourself physically, emotionally, mentally and spiritually.

Index

A

Abdomen 123-126, 137, 205
Abdominal Conditioner 123
Abdominal organs 123
Abdominal pain 179
Abrasions 127, 153
Abscesses 135, 169, 222-223
Accidents 57
Aches and pains 16, 107
Acid reflux disease 37
Acne 35, 135, 145, 169, 173, 177, 179, 183
Acupuncture points 63, 190
Acute conditions 5, 19, 25, 33-35, 49, 58, 104, 170, 208, 210
Addictive substances 19
Adding Mangosteen to Recipes 97
Adrenals 65
Aging 145, 195
Aging skin 145
All at Once 21
Allergic responses 179, 235
Allergies 9, 37, 203, 230, 234, 247
Allergy 12, 234-235
Allergy to mangosteen 12, 234
Aloe vera 191-193
Amalgam fillings 209
Anal tissue 163
Analgesic 6, 114, 131-133, 154-155, 177, 193, 207-208, 222
Analgesic effect 154-155, 207-208
Analgesic Ointment 131
Anti-cancer *i*
Anti-depressant *i*

Anti-fungal *i*, 35, 60, 159, 226
Anti-histamine 129
Anti-histiminic *i*, 8, 35, 170, 186
Anti-inflammatory i, 8, 126, 129, 159, 164, 186, 193, 205, 221, 226
Anti-oxidant *i*
Anti-oxidants 61
Anti-Stress Procedure 53
Anti-ulcer *i*
Anti-viral *i*, 35, 60, 193
Antibacterial *i*, 60, 193
Antibiotics 203, 236
Antiseptic 35, 129, 154, 170, 179, 207, 218, 221, 226
Anus 189
Appetite 86, 90, 95
Arthritis 37, 131, 135, 138, 157, 159, 173, 179
Asian healers *i*, 80
Asthma 37, 104-105, 179
Astringent 6, 81, 114, 122, 127-128, 155, 179
Astringent and Aftershave 127
Astringent lotion 81
Atherosclerosis 37
Athlete's foot 157, 159, 197
Athletes 1, 24, 49
Athletic injuries 106, 173, 179
Athletic performance 106
Auto-Distribution Dose 201
Auto-immune conditions 69

B

Babies 60, 84, 103-104, 111, 162
Babies and toddlers 60, 103
Back pain 33, 131
Bacteria 87
Bad breath 209, 233
Bad eating habits 85
Bee stings 153-154, 169
Behavioral challenges 104
Bentonite clay 136
Bites 35, 127, 129, 153-154, 169-170, 173, 176-177, 191
Bladder 33, 64-65, 189, 230
Bladder infection 33, 64
Bleeding 129, 153, 155-156, 234
Blisters 157, 173, 175
Bloating 203, 206, 234
Blood sugar levels 14, 68
Blotchy 145
Blows and bruises 153, 155
Body odor 143, 233
Boils 169, 173, 175, 233
Bowel and rectal conditions 217
Bowel disorders 37
Bowel regularity 126, 230
Brain 213
Breastfeeding 104
Brittle and broken nails 171
Bronchitis 33, 37, 179
Bruises 127, 129, 153, 155, 169, 173
Budget 27, 29, 63
Burns 127, 129, 153, 155, 183, 191
Burns and scalds 127

C

Caffeine craving 30
Calcium *ii*
Calloused skin 161
Calluses 145, 147, 157
Cancer *i*, 68, 73, 209, 213, 217
Cancer in the mouth 209
Cancer of the bowel, colon or rectum 217
Candidiasis 203
Canker sores 173, 177
Carpal tunnel syndrome 131, 173, 179
Cats 107-109
Cells 8, 13, 22, 28, 45, 48, 55, 67, 69, 95, 198, 202, 214, 241, 245-246
Cellular communication 8
Cellular function 8
Cellular health 23
Centeredness 202
Chaffing 183, 191
Change 11, 31, 38, 45, 48, 51, 66, 69, 72-73, 91, 210
Changing needs 31
Chapped lips 191
Chemical poisoning 11
Chemical sensitivity 141
Chemical toxicity 213
Chi 63-64
Chicken pox 183
Children 5, 1, 16, 24, 59, 60, 77, 81, 83, 84, 97, 101, 102, 103, 104, 105, 106, 111, 114, 137, 180
Chinese Body Clock Procedure 63
Chinese Medicine 65, 126, 238
Chlorine 28
Cholesterol *i*, 37

INDEX

Chronic conditions 5, 13-15, 19, 37-42, 45, 49, 53, 64, 79, 81, 104-105, 108, 131, 170, 206, 210, 241
Circulation 8, 65, 123, 172, 182, 186, 230
Clarity 50, 85, 106, 215, 231, 239, 243
Clay 6, 135-138, 175
Cleansing reaction 9, 11, 50, 89-90, 93, 95, 215, 233-239, 242
Cleansing reactions *iii*, 6, 10, 13, 17, 87, 95, 233, 235, 236, 237, 238, 239, 242, 245
Clearer thinking 239
Cold sores 33, 191
Colitis 37, 126, 203
Common cold 33, 106, 213
Common cold symptoms 213
Constipation 123, 126, 203, 206
Contagious illness 59, 103
Contagious rashes 186
Cotton balls 155, 165
Cough 5, 33, 233, 236
Cramps 57, 167, 189
Cravings 19
Creative visualization 53
Creativity 16, 31, 239
Crohn's disease 203
Cuticle Care 139
Cuticles 139-140, 171, 173, 176
Cuts 127, 153, 155
Cycles 16, 23, 51, 63, 67, 95, 231, 246
Cystitis 79, 81, 102

D

Dandruff 187
Debilitation 12
Deep breathing 53, 87
Deficiencies 15-16

Dehydrated 9, 13, 235
Dehydrated cells 13
Dehydration 11, 35, 234-236
Dental work 221-222
Deodorant 141
Depression 37, 213, 231
Dermatitis 35, 121, 127-129, 161-162, 177, 179
Deteriorating symptoms 42
Detoxification 5, 85, 87, 93-95, 143, 203, 205-206, 213-215, 233, 236, 242, 247
Detoxification crisis 205
Detoxification Program 93
Diabetes 11, 14, 37, 68
Diabetics 14
Diaper rash 183
Diarrhea 79-81, 102, 179, 203, 233
Digestive tract 25, 230
Disharmony 22
Diverticulitis 37, 179, 203, 217
Dogs 109-111
Dreams 239
Drinking Applications 1
Dry mouth 209
Dry skin 133, 146, 157, 161, 176
Dry throat 207

E

Earache 33
Earaches 213
Ears 213
Easy Mangosteen Skin Conditioner 195
Eczema 35, 79, 81, 179, 183, 187
Electromagnetic radiation 74
Emotional distress 21
Emotional releases 233
Emphysema 37

Empty stomach 24, 38-40, 42, 90, 102, 108-109
Endometriosis 131
Endurance 49, 231
Enema 203
Energy 7-9, 16, 22, 54, 63-64, 66, 71-74, 123, 126, 156, 175, 202, 231, 239
Energy level 7, 9, 231
Enzymes 211
Equivalents 4, 111
Esophagus 25
Evaluating the Immediate Effects of Mangosteen 7
Exfoliating Lotion 145
Eye infections 149
Eye Poultice 149
Eyelid infections 149
Eyes 5, 8, 54, 72, 110, 149-150, 213
Eyesight 7, 9, 230
Eyestrain 149-150

F

Facial mask 145-146
Fasting 85, 87, 89-90, 93
Fatigue 37, 231, 233
Feet 125, 133, 145, 147, 157-159, 162, 190, 198, 230
Fever 33, 123, 135, 137, 213
Fibromyalgia 37, 131
Fingers 124-125, 133, 158, 172
First Aid 6, 57, 127-128, 153-156, 170, 191
Fissures 217
Flatulence 206
Flu 59, 75, 104, 106, 113, 207, 213, 236
Flu symptoms 75, 106, 207, 213, 236
Fluorine 28

Foot fungus 197
Foot pain 131, 157
Foot Treatment 157
Forehead 137-138, 151
Foul odors 235
Foul smelling urine 234
Free radical inhibitors *i*
Free radicals 8
Fungal infections 159, 173
Fungus 35, 87, 139-140, 157, 197

G

Gall bladder 65, 126
Gargle 207
Gas 125-126, 234
Gastrointestinal upsets 33
Genital organs 189
Gingivitis 173, 209, 215
Giving Mangosteen to Children 103
Giving Mangosteen to Pets 107
Gleet 79, 81
Gonorrhea 79, 81
Gradually Introducing Mangosteen to Your Diet 11
Gratitude 53-55
Grieve, Mrs. M. 129
Gum conditions 173, 176
Gum infections 222-223
Gum inflammation 223

H

Hag nails 171
Hands 124-125, 133, 145, 147, 161-162, 168, 172, 181, 190, 204, 218, 230

252

INDEX

Head 73, 108, 150-151, 188, 207, 213-215
Headache 213, 215
Headaches 135, 137, 149-151, 188, 231, 234, 245
Healing compounds *i*, 1, 5, 15, 16, 24, 25, 28, 35, 38, 40, 51, 55, 57, 67, 68, 69, 71, 75, 76, 77, 79, 80, 102, 104, 107, 121, 126, 146, 147, 150, 154, 155, 156, 159, 170, 173, 174, 176, 181, 186, 189, 190, 192, 198, 199, 202, 205, 218, 219, 221, 222, 226, 235, 236, 243, 245
Healing cycle 21-22, 34, 58, 67, 69
Healing energies 213
Healing energy 8, 54, 71-74, 156, 202
Healing plateau 45
Healing process 156, 246
Health Evaluation Questionnaire 227
Health Index *iii*, 118, 227, 228, 231, 232, 242
Health maintenance 51, 53, 85, 113, 125
Heart *i*, 64-65, 135, 230
Heart disease *i*
Heavy metal poisoning 11, 135, 203, 206, 209, 213-214
Heavy metals 13, 138
Hemorrhoid Treatments 163
Hemorrhoids 163, 189, 217
Herbs 5, 61-62, 98-99, 190, 238
Hernias 189
Herpes 37
High blood pressure 37
High cholesterol 37
HIV 37
Hives 183
Homeopathic remedies 62
Hunger pangs 21
Hyperactivity and ADHD 37
Hypersensitive stomach 11
Hypersensitivity to mangosteen 234
Hypoglycemia 37

J

Iced tea 19, 77, 86, 114
Ideas for using mangosteen rind 101
Illness 19, 23, 59-60, 103, 113, 167, 202, 231, 234, 236
Immune deficiency 68
Immune system 23, 35, 49, 59-60, 65, 68-69, 75, 83, 87, 104, 107, 208, 231, 236
Immune system support 75
Indigestion 25, 64, 245
Indonesian folk healers 5
Infected pierced earring holes 169
Infection 35, 37, 60, 64, 73, 156, 170, 173, 207, 211, 221, 233
Infections 12, 33, 35, 104, 139-140, 149, 159, 173, 189, 203, 205, 209, 215, 222-223, 225
Inflammation 58, 79, 123, 126-127, 131, 138, 149, 155-156, 173, 175, 179, 203, 209, 217, 223
Inflammation of the eyelid 149
Inflammatory bowel disease 37
Influenza 33
Injuries 21, 33, 41, 57, 106, 108, 128, 131, 135, 155, 173, 176, 179
Insect bites 35, 127, 129, 153-154, 169-170, 177
Insulin 14
Intense emotions 21
Intention 66
Internal Application of Mangosteen 199
Interrupting Mangosteen Therapy 67
Intestinal blockages 123, 126
Intestinal conditions 205-206
Intestinal gas 234
Intestinal infections 203, 205
Intestinal inflammation 123
Intestines 123, 204-205, 219

Intuition 59, 84, 106, 108, 235
Intuitive sense 11, 72
Iron *ii*
Irritated or infected moles 169
Irritation 159, 164, 188, 226
Itchiness 35, 37, 188, 197-198
Itchiness between the toes 197
Itching 138, 163, 186, 225
Itchy feet 157
Itchy scalp 187
Itchy skin 191
Itchy toes 197

J

Jaw 110, 222
Joint pain 131, 234, 245
Joints 136, 138, 179

K

Keeping Mangosteen a Family Friend 113
Kidney 65

L

Labia 189, 225-226
Lactic acid 205
Large intestine 65, 125
Libido 231, 239
Life-threatening 39, 41
Liver 65, 126, 138, 183
Liver spots 183

Loading Dose 15
Locating Mangosteen's Healing Target 71
Loose stools 233
Low vitality 167
Lung 7, 9, 65, 135, 179
Lung capacity 7, 9
Lungs 8, 64, 230

M

Maintenance Dose #1 23
Maintenance Dose #2 27
Maintenance Dose #3 29
Malfunctioning organs 179
Mangosteen Clay 135
Mangosteen Decoction 79
Mangosteen Fast #1 85
Mangosteen Fast #2 89
Mangosteen Paste 173
Mangosteen Tea 75
Mangosteen Tonic 83
Mangosteen-water 87, 90-91, 150-151, 184-186, 190, 204-206, 225
Massage 6, 54, 124-126, 167-168, 172, 188, 205, 238
Massage Oil 167
Medications 11, 14, 62, 84
Medicine cups 5, 167, 177, 196
Meditation 53, 247
Memory 215, 231, 239, 243
Menstruation 234
Mental clarity 50, 85, 106, 215, 231, 243
Mental focus 16
Mentrual cramps 189
Mercury 12-13, 73, 138, 214, 221
Mercury poisoning 12, 73
Mercury spots 221
Metabolic wastes 138, 233, 235

INDEX

Minerals 61, 238
Mini-Poultice 169
Minor burns 155, 183, 191
Minor health challenges 23, 29
Minor health conditions 15, 109
Minor wounds 6, 127, 153
Moisturizing lotion 139, 145, 147, 158, 161, 191
Mood swings 106
Morton, Julie F. 80
Mosquito bites 173, 176
Mouth 4-5, 8-9, 13, 19, 54, 62, 71-73, 108-110, 138, 176, 199, 201, 209-211, 213-215, 221-222, 224, 230
Mouth infections 209
Mouth sores 215, 221
Mouthwash 209
Mucus discharge 234
Multiple sclerosis 37
Muscle cramps 167
Muscle spasms 57, 131
Muscle tension 168
Muscles 125, 167

N

Nail cuticles 173, 176
Nail fungus 139
Nail infections 139-140
Nail Treatment 171
Natural cleansing cycles 51
Natural healing methods 238
Neuralgia 131
Nicotine 19
North American Indians 129
Nutritional deficiencies 15
Nutritional deficiency 9
Nutritional supplements *iii*,16,73

O

Oral Detox 213
Organs 25, 55, 63-66, 121, 123, 125-126, 136, 179, 189, 231, 233
Over-the-counter remedies 35
Overweight adults 24
Oxygen 55

P

Pain 21-22, 33, 37, 58, 72, 125, 131, 135, 138, 157, 159, 165, 170, 176, 179, 188, 215, 222-223, 231, 234, 245-246
Pain tolerance 222
Painful areas 126, 176
Pancreas 65
Parasites 12-13, 85, 87, 203, 206
Performance 49-50, 106
Pets 5,1,102,107,110
Phosphorous *ii*
Phytoceutical healing compounds 71
Phytoceuticals *i*
Pimples 145, 169, 183, 234
Pink eye 149
PMS 33
Poison ivy 35, 183, 186
Polysaccharides *i*
Poor food combination 25
Positive cleansing reactions 233, 239, 245
Potassium *ii*
Poultice 179
Prescription medications 11, 14, 62
Probiotic 205
Procedure for Acute Conditions 33
Procedure for Chronic Conditions 37

Procedure for Health Improvement #1 39
Procedure for Health Improvement #2 41
Psoriasis 179, 183
Pulmonary disease 37
Puncture wounds 169

Q

Quinones *i*

R

Rash Plaster 183
Rashes 33, 35, 104, 118, 121-122, 138, 161-162, 183, 186, 191, 234
Recipe ideas 97, 101
Rectal Implant 217
Reducing a dosage 43
Relaxation 53
Reproductive organs 126, 231
Rheumatoid arthritis 37
Rhythm 95-96, 247
Rind 3-5, 12-13, 15-16, 24, 57, 61-62, 78-81, 90, 97-102, 104, 108, 123-124, 126, 128, 133, 135, 141-142, 145-147, 149-151, 154, 156-157, 161, 163, 167, 170-171, 174, 177, 180-181, 184-185, 187-192, 195-198, 201, 204-205, 210-211, 214, 217-219, 221-226
Ringworm 33, 35, 169
Rough 131, 133, 161
Rough, cracked skin 131

S

Saccharomyces boulardii 205
Saliva 202, 211, 214, 222
Scalds 127, 129
Scalp condition 188
Scalp sores 187
Scalp Treatment 187
Scaly skin 145-147, 177
Scars 135, 169-170
Scrapes 127, 153
Sensitive skin 150, 162, 177, 191, 226
Sensitive stomach 12
Sensitivity 7, 72-73, 117, 141, 222, 239
Serious conditions 39, 41-42, 49, 55, 108, 226, 241
Sharing a First Dose with Others 117
Shaving 127
Sick-Day Prevention Dose 59
Sinuses 8, 213
Sinusitis 33, 138, 213
Sipping mangosteen 5, 19-20
Sitz Bath 189
Skin conditions 35, 37, 121, 145-146, 159, 161-162, 168, 175-176, 179, 183, 195
Skin disorders 79, 81
Skin eruptions 183, 187
Skin eruptions on the scalp 187
Skin irritations 183, 191
Skin rashes 234
Skin-care maintenance 195
Small intestine 65
Small scars 169-170
Small wounds 153
Smooth Mangosteen Paste 98, 132-133, 162, 177, 188
Sore throat 33, 75, 77, 173, 176, 207-208
Sore throats 176

INDEX

Sores 33, 173, 177, 179, 187, 191, 209, 215, 221
Sores on the tongue, gums or inside the cheeks 209
Spleen 65
Sprains 131, 179
Stamina 49, 106, 231
Stilbenes *i*
Stomach 11-12, 24-25, 38-40, 42, 64-65, 90, 102, 108-109, 126, 230
Strength 22, 49, 126, 133, 236
Strep throat 207
Stress 5, 19, 29, 53-54, 66, 75, 87, 103-104, 149, 167-168, 201-202, 205, 222, 238, 243, 245-247
Stressed immune system 59
Stressful lives 8
Stressful situation 83-84
Stubborn Conditions 45
Sunburn 6, 122, 140, 183, 186, 191-193
Sunburn Treatment 191
Surgery 57, 83, 135
Swallowing 4, 19-20, 58, 101, 108, 211, 214, 222
Swelling 127, 135, 155, 164, 173, 186
Swellings 129
Swollen glands 75, 176, 207, 234

T

Taking Mangosteen with Herbs and Supplements 61
Tantien 126
Tea 5, 12, 19, 34, 42, 54, 62, 75-80, 86, 89, 91, 114, 208, 238
Teenagers 16, 24, 60, 84, 105
Temples 137, 151
Templeman, J. Frederic, M.D. *i*

Testimonials *i*, *iii*, 3
Throat 25, 33, 75, 77, 108, 173, 176, 207-208, 213-214, 230
Thrush 209, 221
Tired eyes 149
Toddlers 60, 84, 103
Toe Treatment 197
Toenail conditions 197
Tonic 5, 25, 75, 83-84, 103-104, 106, 114
Tonsillitis 75, 207
Tooth and Gum Compress 221
Tooth and Gum Pack 223
Tooth decay 211
Tooth infection 221
Tooth pain 223
Toothache 33, 209, 215, 221
Top Dose Procedure 49
Topical Applications 121
Topical infections 173
Toxicity 11-12, 213
Toxin release 9
Toxins 9-10, 13, 28, 35, 49, 73, 87, 135, 138, 143, 175, 202, 205, 210-211, 214-215, 219, 233, 235, 238, 246
Traditional remedies 219
Trauma Dose 57
Traumatic experience 57
Treats for cats and dogs 109
Triple warmer 65-66
Tumors 129, 135-136, 173, 175-176, 179

U

Underlying problem 38
Undiluted 5, 28, 30, 34, 85, 87, 150, 214
Urethra 79, 189

V

Vagina 189, 225-226
Vaginal itching 225
Vaginal Wipe 225
Vaginal yeast infections 189
Varicose veins 129
Viruses 87
Visual acuity 7
Vitality 21, 35, 54, 74, 167
Vitamin B1 *ii*
Vitamin B2 *ii*
Vitamin B6 *ii*
Vitamin C *ii*
Vitamins *ii*, 61,205,238

W

Warts 169-170
Water 4-5, 12-13, 15, 24, 27-28, 30, 34-35, 42, 61-62, 72, 75-77, 79-81, 85-87, 89-91, 104, 109, 114, 143, 146, 150-151, 154-155, 174-175, 180-181, 184-186, 188-190, 204-206, 214-215, 218-219, 225-226, 233, 235-236, 238
Weak joints 179
Weight loss 86, 90
Well-being 38, 50, 85, 239, 242, 246
Witch hazel 128-129
Withdrawal symptoms 57
Wounds 6, 35, 127, 153, 169, 179

X

Xanthones *i*

Y

Yeast 12-13, 33, 37, 87, 189, 205, 225
Yeast infection 37
Yeast infections 12, 33, 189, 225
Your First Dose 3, 5, 7, 9, 45, 73, 118, 234, 235
Your mangosteen story 118
Your Top Dose 50